Lernkrimi Englisch

W0053228

Blood and Breakfast

Andrew Ridley
Alison Romer

compact

Weitere Informationen zu Compact Lernkrimis finden Sie am Ende des Buches und unter www.lernkrimi.de.

© Compact Verlag GmbH
Baierbrunner Straße 27, 81379 München
Ausgabe 2017

Redaktion: Helga Aichele
Fachkorrektur: Fiona Cain
Produktion: Ute Hausleiter
Titelillustration: Karl Knospe
Lernkrimi-Logo: Carsten Abelbeck
Gestaltung: EKH Werbeagentur GbR, textum GmbH
Umschlaggestaltung: red.sign GbR, Stuttgart; Hartmut Baier

ISBN 978-3-8174-1385-0
381741385/1

www.compactverlag.de, www.lernkrimi.de, www.facebook.com/lernkrimi

 # Vorwort

Liebe Leserin, lieber Leser,

sicher zum Lernerfolg – mit Spaß und Spannung! Die Compact Lernkrimis mit ihrer Kombination aus Lektüre und didaktischem Übungsanteil eignen sich hervorragend, um breite Sprachkompetenzen in der Fremdsprache zu erwerben. Der Lernende wird dabei durch die spannende Handlung, das angemessene Sprachniveau und den stetig ansteigenden Schwierigkeitsgrad der Übungen gefördert und motiviert.

Entwickelt nach neuesten Erkenntnissen der Fremdsprachendidaktik, sind Compact Lernkrimis das ideale Medium für einen Lernerfolg im Selbststudium. Durch die kleinen Texteinheiten und den hohen Übungsanteil sind sie aber auch als Unterrichtslektüre bestens geeignet.

So lernen Sie mit Compact Lernkrimis:
- **Mit Begeisterung lernen:** Die packende Krimihandlung motiviert Sie beim Lesen des englischen Originaltextes.
- **Wissen intensivieren und erweitern:** Durch die Kombination aus didaktisch aufbereiteter Lektüre und textbezogenen Übungen testen und trainieren Sie Ihre Sprachkenntnisse effektiv. Vokabelangaben auf jeder Seite unterstützen Sie beim Lesen.
- **Systematisch lernen:** Knüpfen Sie an Ihr individuelles Sprachniveau an und setzen Sie sich eigene Lernziele.
- **Unabhängig sein:** Lernen Sie individuell – wo und wann immer Sie wollen.

Viel Spaß beim **spannenden Erlernen der englischen Sprache**
wünscht Ihnen

Prof. Dr. Christiane Neveling
Didaktik der romanischen Sprachen, Universität Leipzig

Inhalt

Blood and Breakfast

Andrew Ridley

A Shot in the Night

How good it is to be on holiday with my daughter, thinks Detective Inspector Rush. He is happy to be away from his job in Leeds in the north of England for a few days. His job is very important to him, but he also likes to spend time with his daughter, Sally. A week in Kent[i] on the south east coast will be **enjoyable** for both of them.

enjoyable	vergnüglich
view	Aussicht; Sicht
pleased	erfreut

"Drive a little slower, Dad," says Sally. "You aren't driving a police car now. I would like to enjoy the **view**. It's so beautiful."

They are driving along the coast road between Folkestone and Hastings and there is a beautiful view of the sea.

"Okay," says her father. "We have a few hours yet. We must arrive in time for the evening meal, though."

They are quiet for a few minutes, and then he speaks again.

"I'm so **pleased** that you have come on holiday with me," he says. "There are not many 24-year-old daughters who want to go on holiday with their fathers."

"No," she laughs. "You really are very lucky to have me with you."

He laughs as well. "Yes, I know I am. It's so long since we spent some time together. I think that the last time was two years ago. Then we went on the Aikido course in Birmingham. I'm

Kent ist die südöstlichste Grafschaft Englands. Neben der bekannten Küste prägen auch viele Obstgärten und Hopfenfelder die Landschaft, weshalb Kent auch „Garten Englands" genannt wird.

sorry that I always seem to be so **busy**."

"Don't worry about it, Dad," she replies. "It makes the time that we do spend together really special."

"Thanks," he answers. "I'm really looking forward to this week.

busy	beschäftigt
especially	besonders
amazing	erstaunlich
proudly	stolz
handsome	attraktiv, gutaussehend
bay	Bucht

Especially the open-air classical concert at Leeds Castle. That should be really good."

"Yes," she agrees. "The 1812 Overture with real cannons and fireworks should be **amazing**."

After a moment, she asks, "Do you know why it's called Leeds Castle? It can't be anything to do with the city of Leeds where we live, can it?"

"No," replies her father, "it isn't. I read somewhere that the Saxons called the area 'Esledes'. Over the years it became 'Leeds'."

"You're so clever, Dad," says Sally, **proudly**. "Sometimes I think that you know everything."

Detective Inspector Rush smiles, but says nothing.

> Typisch britisch! Ein **Bed and Breakfast** (B and B) findet sich fast in jedem Ort. Diese Gästezimmer bei Privatleuten oder Frühstückspensionen sind individueller als Hotels und bieten hausgemachtes Frühstück und Insidertipps für Reisende.

Sally looks at her father. He is 47 years old, but he looks younger. His brown hair has some grey at the sides. He is not **handsome**, she thinks, but he is good-looking. He is also still a fit man. They used to do Aikido together, but now her father practises yoga.

Twenty minutes later they drive past St Mary's **Bay** and after a few hundred metres see a sign at the side of the road.

"Littlestone Farm, Bed and Breakfast," ⓘ reads Sally. "That's it."

Exercise 1: True or false? Kreuzen Sie die richtigen Aussagen an!

1. Sally's father is a policeman in the North of England. ☐
2. They are travelling by bus. ☐
3. They will go to a rock concert at Leeds Castle. ☐
4. DI Rush is old and ugly. ☐
5. He does not spend a lot of time with his daughter. ☐
6. Sally and her father do yoga together. ☐
7. Leeds Castle is in the city of Leeds. ☐

DI Rush turns left down a narrow lane. He drives slowly, as the road is uneven. After a few minutes they arrive in the yard of a small farm. There is a house with a thatched roof, and a barn stands at the end of the yard. DI Rush parks his car at the side of it. They both climb out of the car and stretch. A dog is barking and as they turn towards the house, the door opens. A man dressed in old jeans and a dirty, blue shirt stands in the doorway. He is about forty years old, small and wiry with brown hair. As they approach, Sally can see that his eyes are a beautiful blue.

"Good afternoon," he says. "Mr Rush, is it?" He holds out a grubby hand. "I'm Alan, Alan Larkin."

lane	schmaler Weg, Gasse
uneven	uneben
yard	Hof
thatched	reetgedeckt
barn	Scheune
doorway	Türöffnung
wiry	drahtig
to approach	sich nähern
grubby	dreckig, schmuddelig

They **shake hands**.

"And you must be Sally," he says as he turns towards her.

She shakes his hand **reluctantly**, because she doesn't like the fact that it is dirty.

"Come inside," he says. "Brenda will make you a cup of tea, and then you can bring in your cases and **unpack**."

to shake hands	sich die Hand geben
reluctantly	widerwillig
to unpack	auspacken
hall	Flur
settee	Sofa
surprised	überrascht
tidy	ordentlich
to appear	(er)scheinen
just	*hier*: gerade eben
vegetarian	Vegetarier(in)

They follow him into the house.

"How was your journey here?" he asks.

He doesn't wait for an answer, but calls, "Brenda, Mr Rush and his daughter are here."

DI Rush and Sally walk behind him down the **hall** and into the living room. There are two large **settees**, a television, a dining table with six chairs and other pieces of furniture. Sally is **surprised** to see that the room is clean and **tidy**.

Not like Mr Larkin, she thinks.

Brenda **appears** from the kitchen. She looks a little older than Mr Larkin and is also a few inches taller. She is quite large and has a round face with red cheeks. She wipes her hands on a towel before she shakes their hands.

"I'm **just** making the evening meal," she says. "I hope you like meat and potato pie."

"Yes, that will be fine, Mrs Larkin," says DI Rush. "Sally used to be a **vegetarian**, but she started to eat meat again last year."

> **Meat and potato pie** ist ein typisches Auflaufgericht aus Fleischstücken, Gemüse und Kartoffeln.

"Please call me Brenda, Mr Rush," she says. "Well, I'm sure you'll enjoy my pie, Sally. Everyone does. Now sit down and I'll bring you both a nice cup of tea. You must be ready for a drink after driving all that way."

She goes back into the kitchen and Mr Larkin follows her.

I wish that my mother and father were still together, thinks Sally. DI Rush has been in the police for twenty-five years. Twelve years ago he became a detective inspector, and two years later her mother left him because he was never at home. He was always working.

tray	Tablett
to pour	(ein)gießen
unlike	anders als

Since then, Sally has lived with her mother. I love them both, she thinks. Sometimes life is so difficult.

They sit on the settee and look around at the pictures on the walls.

"What do you think so far?" asks the inspector.

"Well, it's not The Ritz, but it seems okay," replies Sally. "Mr Larkin looks a bit grubby, though. I'm glad he's not cooking our evening meal."

They both laugh.

Just then Mr Larkin comes through the kitchen door. Behind him is Mrs Larkin with a tray in her hands. She places the cups and teapot on the table.

"Did you have a good journey here?" she asks as she pours the tea.

"Yes, thank you," answers DI Rush, as unlike Mr Larkin, Mrs Larkin waits for an answer.

When they all have a cup of tea, Mr Larkin asks, "What job do you do, Mr Rush?"

"Please, call me David," replies DI Rush. "I work in a bank, the same as Sally," he lies.

10

When he is on holiday, he never tells people that he is a policeman. People always want to talk about police work or complain about the police.

"Is this actually[i] a farm or do you just have the bed and breakfast business?" he asks.

"The only animal we have here is a dog," replies Mrs Larkin. "I run the bed and breakfast. Alan has

a large van. He carries things about for people. It brings in a little extra money."

"What kind of dog do you have?" asks Sally. "I like dogs."

"I don't think you would like Brutus," says Mrs Larkin. "He's a large Rottweiler and he's not very friendly. We keep him locked in the backyard when we have visitors."

to complain	sich beklagen
to run (a business)	*hier*: (einen Betrieb) führen
van	Lieferwagen
drawer	Schublade
en suite bathroom	eigenes Bad

They continue talking until they have finished their tea. Then Mr Larkin helps DI Rush to bring in the suitcases from the car. He takes them up to their rooms. Both rooms are at the front of the house and look out onto the yard. In each room is a single bed, a wardrobe with drawers and a chair. Each room also has an en suite bathroom with a shower.

"If you want to go for a walk before dinner, the beach is not far from here," says Mr Larkin. "If you go down the path between the house and the barn, you'll arrive at the sea in twenty minutes."

"Thanks," answers DI Rush. "It would be nice to go for a walk. My legs are stiff after the journey from Leeds."

Exercise 2: Questions about the text. Beantworten Sie die Fragen zum Text in ganzen Sätzen!

1. How have Sally and her father travelled to Kent?

   _____

2. Why does Sally shake Mr Larkin's hand reluctantly?

   _____

3. Who comes out of the kitchen?

   _____

4. Where does DI Rush say that he works?

   _____

5. What is Mrs Larkin doing in the kitchen?

   _____

6. Who is Brutus?

   _____

DI Rush unpacks his case and hangs his clothes in the old, wooden wardrobe. After a hot shower, he feels **refreshed**. When he has dressed in blue jeans, a blue **short-sleeved** shirt and a **leather** jacket, he knocks on Sally's door. She is still in the shower, however. Just like her mother, he thinks to himself and smiles. She used to take hours to get herself ready to go out. He goes down into the living room to wait for her.

refreshed	erfrischt, erholt
short-sleeved	kurzärmelig
leather	Leder

He looks up from the newspaper that he is reading when Sally eventually comes down the stairs. She is also wearing blue jeans, but she has on a yellow T-shirt. Her long, blonde hair is tied back in a ponytail.

"Are you sure that you'll be warm enough?" asks her father. "It may be windy down by the sea."

"Of course I'll be warm enough, Dad. You worry too much," she laughs.

They leave the house and follow the path between the house and the barn. It goes through fields and a small wood. When they come out of the wood, they can see the sea.

"Oh, the English Channel," says Sally. "Can you see France?"

"I can see something," replies her father, "but it's probably just a low cloud."

eventually	schließlich
to tie	binden
ponytail	Pferdeschwanz
English Channel	Ärmelkanal
steep	steil
pebble	Kieselstein
Is anything the matter?	Stimmt etwas nicht?
strange	seltsam

They walk on in the evening sunlight to the top of the cliff. Then they stop for a moment to look at the sea and watch the large ships out on the water.

"Shall we go down to the beach?" asks Sally and begins to go down the steep path. DI Rush follows her carefully.

"Not too fast," he calls. "My legs are older than yours."

They spend some time on the beach, where they walk by the sea and throw pebbles into the water. Then they climb back up the path.

"You're very quiet, Dad," says Sally. "Is anything the matter?"

"Not really," he replies. "I was just thinking that the path from the farm is very easy to follow. It looks as though lots of people use it. I think that's strange when there are only a few guests each week."

He bends and picks up a cigarette packet from the ground.

"French cigarettes," he says. "Perhaps they have had French guests."

"Really, Dad," laughs Sally. "Don't you ever stop being a detective? I have a friend who smokes Russian cigarettes and she's not Russian."

They make their way back to the farm, and as they enter the yard, they see that a large, new BMW is parked in front of the barn. As they go into the house, Mrs Larkin is serving the evening meal.

just in time	gerade (noch) rechtzeitig
slim	schlank
wrist	Handgelenk
to clear the table	den Tisch abräumen
to wonder	sich fragen
gunshot	(Gewehr-)Schuss
to switch on/off	an-/ausschalten

There is already a man sitting at the dining table.

"Hello, you two," calls Mrs Larkin. "You're just in time. This is Mr Dalton. He's staying here for the night."

DI Rush and Sally introduce themselves to Mr Dalton. He is about thirty years of age, slim and has short, blonde hair. He is dressed in an expensive suit, and the inspector sees that he has a Rolex watch on his wrist.

Sally thinks he is quite good-looking, and during the meal, she tries to talk to him. Mr Dalton, however, doesn't want to talk.

He answers her questions with "yes" or "no" and eventually she gives up and talks to her father instead.

After the meal, Mr Dalton goes upstairs to his room. Mrs Larkin clears the table and returns to the kitchen.

"Mr Dalton doesn't say very much, does he?" says Sally when they are alone.

"No," replies her father. "He didn't want to talk about himself, did he? I wonder what his job is. That was a very expensive Rolex that he had on his wrist, and new BMWs aren't cheap."

"Well, I don't think we're going to find out," says Sally. "Mrs Larkin said that he's only here for one night."

They sit on the settee. Sally watches the television and DI Rush reads a book that he has brought with him.

At 9 p.m. Mrs Larkin makes a cup of tea for them, and at 10 p.m. they decide to go to bed. They are both tired after the journey. DI Rush lies awake for a little while. He thinks about what they will do in the morning. He also thinks about Mr Dalton. Why is a man with so much money at a bed and breakfast?

He should be in a four-star hotel, thinks DI Rush as he falls asleep.

Exercise 3: Odd one out. Markieren Sie das nicht in die Reihe passende Wort!

1. our   week   month   minute

2. settee   dining table   chair   furniture

3. wardrobe   bed   drawer   yard

4. hand   eye   pie   cheek

5. shirt   case   jacket   jeans

It is still dark when he suddenly wakes up. He is sure that the noise that woke him was a gunshot. He switches on the lamp at the side of his bed and looks at the clock. Half past three. He switches off the lamp again and gets out of bed. He looks out of his window, but the yard below is completely black. Since he is awake, he decides to get up and have a look outside. He puts on his trousers, shoes and a jumper and quietly goes down the stairs. He **unlocks** and opens the front door.

Suddenly, the light in the hall is switched on.

"It's a little early to be going out for a walk, isn't it, Mr Rush?" says a voice behind him.

DI Rush's heart is **beating** like a **drum**. He turns and sees that Mr Larkin has come out of the living room. Behind him stands a large, black Rottweiler. The dog **growls** deeply when DI Rush looks at it.

to unlock	aufschließen
to beat	schlagen
drum	Trommel
to growl	knurren
poacher	Wilderer
to be about	*hier*: in der Gegend sein
injured	verletzt
bullet	Kugel
lounge	Wohnzimmer

"Be quiet, Brutus!" says Larkin.

The dog stops growling, but it doesn't take its eyes off DI Rush.

"Something woke me," says the detective. "It sounded like a gunshot."

"Yes, I heard it, too," says Mr Larkin. "I was in the living room. I must have fallen asleep while I was watching the television."

"What do you think it was?" asks the DI.

"It's probably **poachers**," replies Larkin. "They are often around here at night. Don't go out when they **are about**. You could be **injured** or even killed. You wouldn't be the first person to be killed by a poacher's **bullet**."

"No," he replies. "You're probably right. I think I'll go back to bed and see if I can sleep."

DI Rush starts to climb the stairs and then turns to look back. Mr Larkin has returned to the **lounge**, but Brutus is standing there watching him with cold, black eyes.

Blood on the Ground

At breakfast that morning, only Sally and her father are at the table.

"Where's Mr Dalton?" asks Sally when Mrs Larkin comes from the kitchen.

"Oh, he was up very early," she replies. "He had to catch a ferry

ferry	Fähre
to redden	rot werden
fried egg	Spiegelei
poached	*hier*: pochiert

to France. He needed to be in Paris for a meeting this morning."

"Why didn't he fly?" asks the inspector.

"He needed his car with him," replies Mrs Larkin quickly, and her cheeks begin to redden. "Now, what can I get you for breakfast?"

"A full English breakfast [i] for me," says the inspector. "Could I have a fried egg, please?"

"And for me, two poached eggs on toast, please," says Sally.

When Mrs Larkin returns to the kitchen, they both look at each other.

"It's strange that Mr Dalton left so early for the ferry. If he needed his car in Paris, he could have gone on the Eurotunnel train with it," says the inspector.

"Perhaps he likes to drive," Sally replies. "He left early. I heard his car in the yard when it was still dark. It woke me."

"I didn't hear that," says her father, "but I did hear something else."

Das warme **Full English Breakfast** mit Spiegelei, gebratenem Speck, Tomaten usw. ist v.a. bei Urlaubern beliebt. Im Alltag essen es die wenigsten Briten.

He then tells her about the shot that he heard in the night.

"Really?" **gasps** Sally. "You don't think that had anything to do with Mr Dalton leaving early, do you?"

"I hope not," answers her father. "And Mr Larkin said it was poachers?" Sally continues. "That's terrible. I **hate** to think that people go around with guns and kill poor animals in the middle of the night. The world would be a better place without guns."

to gasp	keuchen, nach Luft schnappen
to hate	hassen
to add	hinzufügen
mushroom	Pilz

They stop talking as Mrs Larkin returns from the kitchen. She places a plate in front of the inspector.

"Here's your full English breakfast, David," she says. "And here are your poached eggs on toast, Sally. I hope they're not too hard," she **adds** as she puts a plate in front of Sally.

"That smells delicious," says the inspector as he looks at his plate full of food: two eggs, bacon, **mushrooms**, beans and fried bread. "I'll need a long walk after this," he continues. "After a week here, I'll be fat. Your cooking is really excellent, Brenda."

She smiles and goes back into the kitchen.

A few seconds later she appears again with a pot of tea. She places it on the table and then leaves them alone.

DI Rush and Sally eat their breakfast. They discuss how they will spend their day. It is a beautiful morning with a blue sky and warm sunshine. They decide to visit Canterbury, as they have never been there. They would both like to see the famous cathedral.

When Mrs Larkin returns to clear the table, they talk with her about Canterbury. Finally, DI Rush asks where Mr Larkin is.

"He had to leave early as well," she replies. "He's gone up to London to see someone about some business."

Before he can ask anything else, Mrs Larkin hurries off into the kitchen.

Sally and her father go upstairs to their rooms and pack a small rucksack each. Sally goes out into the yard and sees her father near the barn door. As she walks towards him, she **slips**. She looks down and sees a small **pool** of red **liquid**. She bends down to look at it, and her father comes over to her.

"What is it, Dad?" she asks. "It looks like blood to me."

Her father puts his finger into

to slip	ausrutschen
pool	*hier*: Lache
liquid	Flüssigkeit
to examine	untersuchen
rabbit	Kaninchen
to disappear	verschwinden
silence	Stille
to shrug one's shoulders	mit den Achseln zucken

the liquid and **examines** it. "I think you're right," he says. "What's a pool of blood doing here in the yard?"

"Brutus caught a **rabbit** this morning and brought it into the yard," says Mrs Larkin.

She is standing behind them with a bucket of water.

"I'm sorry that you had to see that," she continues. "I was going to clean it up earlier, but I was busy in the kitchen."

She pours the water onto[i] the blood to wash it away. When she is happy that all of the blood has **disappeared**, she goes back into[i] the house.

Die Präpositionen **onto** und **into** werden zusammen mit Bewegungsverben verwenden. Sie geben eine Richtung an oder das Ergebnis einer Bewegung: *She pours water onto the blood.* Sie gießt Wasser auf das Blut (drauf).

Sally and her father stand in **silence**. They look at each other and he **shrugs his shoulders**.

"I thought they locked Brutus in the backyard," Sally says.

"That's what Mrs Larkin said yesterday," agrees her father.

"Perhaps the poachers are not the only killers around here **after dark**. I don't like to think that Brutus is walking about freely at night."

"Oh, don't think about it, then,"

| after dark | nach Einbruch der Dunkelheit |
| pleasant | erfreulich |

says Sally. "Let's go and have a nice day in Canterbury."

Exercise 4: Translation. Übersetzen Sie die Begriffe ins Englische!

1. Spiegelei _____

2. Pilz _____

3. hinzufügen _____

4. Gewehr _____

5. Tablett _____

6. sich beklagen _____

7. ordentlich _____

They spend a **pleasant** day in Canterbury. They visit the castle and the cathedral, and they have lunch at one of the cafés in the town centre. They also look around the shops, before they return to their car and drive back to Littlestone Farm.

On their return, Mr Larkin is standing at the door of the house.

"Did you have a good time in Canterbury?" he asks.

"Yes, we did, thanks," replies DI Rush. "How was London?"

"Too busy and too noisy," Larkin laughs.

"Did you drive there?" asks the DI.

"Yes," Larkin answers cautiously. "Why?"

"It's just that your van was still in the barn this morning," answers the DI.

The smile disappears from Larkin's face and his cold, blue eyes turn towards DI Rush.

"I walked to the end of the lane and a friend took me in his car," he says after a moment.

"Oh, right," replies DI Rush.

"Any more questions?" he asks sharply.

cautiously	vorsichtig
suspicious	misstrauisch, verdächtig
obviously	offensichtlich

"No, Alan," answers the inspector. "None at all."

Larkin turns and disappears into the house.

Sally and the inspector look at each other, before they follow him through the door. They go upstairs to their rooms to wash before the evening meal.

Tonight they are the only two at the table. While they eat, Sally and the inspector discuss their day in Canterbury, but both of them are thinking about the strange things that have happened since they arrived at Littlestone Farm.

Mrs Larkin serves their food but doesn't say much this evening. Mr Larkin is nowhere to be seen.

After the meal, Sally watches TV again, while her father reads his book. When they go upstairs, they both go into Sally's room.

"Something's not right here," says DI Rush after she has closed the door. "I think I'll stay awake tonight and see if anything happens."

"Oh, Dad," says Sally. "You're not at work now. Just go to bed."

"Sorry, Sally," he replies. "I have a suspicious mind. I just want to see if anything happens during the night here."

"Well, be careful, Dad," Sally warns. "There are obviously people out there at night with guns."

"Don't worry. I can take care of myself," says her father before he goes to his room.

He takes off his shoes and lies on the bed. He **sets** his alarm clock for 2 a.m. and then closes his eyes.

Exercise 5: Match-up. Welche Wörter haben eine ähnliche Bedeutung? Ordnen Sie zu!

1. ☐ answer   **a)** enjoyable

2. ☐ grubby   **b)** cautiously

3. ☐ carefully   **c)** attractive

4. ☐ handsome   **d)** reply

5. ☐ pleasant   **e)** dirty

He only seems to have slept for seconds when the alarm wakes him. After he stops the alarm, he lies for a few minutes on the bed. Then he gets up, goes to the open window and looks out. The yard is completely dark and there is no sound at all.

He sits by the window and the hours go by. The only sounds he hears are a dog barking somewhere and also an **owl** in the wood. When it starts to become light, he undresses and gets into bed, where he soon falls asleep.

At breakfast the next morning, he tells Sally about his night.

"Perhaps you are too suspicious, Dad," she says. "I think it's the fact that you're a policeman that makes you **suspect** everyone. Don't you think?"

to set	*hier*: stellen
owl	Eule
to suspect	verdächtigen

22

"You could be right," her father agrees. "I think that I should leave my work behind for a week and just enjoy my holiday. The weather is beautiful and the food is great."

"And, of course, the company is wonderful," Sally adds and she laughs.

"Indeed it is," agrees her father and he laughs, too.

They spend the day in Ramsgate on the coast. It is some distance away, but DI Rush had a holiday there when he was a teenager and wants to go back. He finds that he cannot really remember much. Everything is more modern now. However, they have a pleasant day. They do all the things that DI Rush used to do when he was a teenager on holiday. They walk by the sea, eat fish and chips and go to the fairground. They go on the rides, and at one of the stalls, DI Rush wins a bar of chocolate by throwing darts. They have

company	Gesellschaft
indeed	wirklich, in der Tat
to remember	sich erinnern
fairground	Rummelplatz
stall	Stand
bar	*hier*: Riegel
dart	Wurfpfeil
cloth	Tuch, Lappen

both eaten enough, so he puts it in his pocket for later.

For Sally it is a new experience. She has spent all her holidays in Spain or France. She has never had a holiday on the coast in England.

When they arrive back at Littlestone Farm, Mr Larkin is in the barn. The doors are open, and they can see him in the back of his van. He has a bucket and a cloth. He looks up as they get out of the car. They are both laughing.

"You've obviously had a good day," he says. "It must be nice to have no work to do."

Exercise 6: Pronouns. Schreiben Sie die Sätze neu und ersetzen sie den markierten Satzteil mit dem passenden Pronomen!

1. **DI Rush** likes Brenda's cooking.

   _____

2. **Sally and her father** follow **Mr Larkin** through the door.

   _____

3. **Mrs Larkin** serves **the food** in silence.

   _____

4. **DI Rush** goes to Ramsgate with **his daughter.**

   _____

"It is very nice indeed," replies DI Rush. "Are you going out with the van this evening, Alan?"

"No," Larkin answers sharply. "I just thought that I should clean it out. Then it will be ready when I need it again."

He turns away and begins to clean the floor.

DI Rush looks at Sally and shrugs his shoulders. They walk across the yard and into the house. Mrs Larkin is obviously in the kitchen, and the smell of the evening meal fills the hall.

"It smells like roast lamb," says Sally. "The meals here really are delicious."

"I can hardly believe that you used to be a vegetarian," her father laughs.

roast	gebraten
hardly	kaum
to believe	glauben

Apparently, they are still the only guests at the house. While they eat their evening meal, they talk together. They also speak to Mrs Larkin when she appears from the kitchen to serve the food.

They tell her about their visit to Ramsgate and DI Rush's holiday there years ago. When they have eaten, they decide to sit in the garden to drink their coffee. It is a beautiful evening, and they watch the sun disappear behind the wood.

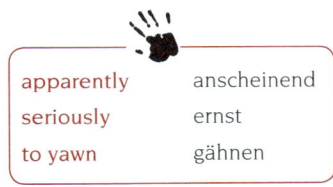

apparently	anscheinend
seriously	ernst
to yawn	gähnen

"Two days gone already," says Sally. "I can't believe how quickly the time goes by."

"Yes, it will soon be time to pack our cases," replies her father.

"Well, Mrs Larkin is okay, and I really like her meals," says Sally, "but I'm not sure about Mr Larkin. Sometimes I think he is okay, and at other times I feel that there's something suspicious about him."

"I think that we both agree on that," the inspector laughs. Then he continues more seriously. "You know what I said this morning, about forgetting police work for a week. Well, I still think Mr Larkin is doing something illegal. I think I might stay awake again tonight."

"Well, I think that you should go to sleep tonight. You have been yawning all day today," says Sally.

They go inside and watch television together for an hour. Then they go up to their rooms.

"Are you really going to stay awake tonight, Dad?" Sally asks, as she goes into her room.

"I don't know," replies her father. "As you said, I should really sleep tonight. I might set my alarm and just get up for a short time to see if anything is happening."

Sally smiles. She knows that her father will get up during the night. He has been a detective for too many years now. If he thinks there is something suspicious going on, then he will not be able **to get a good night's sleep**.

"Good night, Dad," she smiles. "Sleep well."

Exercise 7: Synonyms. Lesen Sie weiter und finden Sie die Synonyme zu den angegebenen Ausdrücken im Text!

noises   night bird   return   silent   vehicle

possibly

At 2 a.m. DI Rush is waiting by his open window. He sits there for thirty minutes, and once again the only sounds that he hears are the barking of the dog and the call of the owl. He is about to go back to bed when he hears someone swear quietly. He puts his head out of the window, but everything is quiet again. With his head out of the window, he can see that there is a light on in the barn. Perhaps Larkin is working on his van, he thinks. However, there is no sound at all. He thinks for a few seconds and then decides to go and see what is happening in the barn. Probably Larkin didn't switch the light off, the inspector tells himself.

He goes quietly down the stairs. The house is dark and silent. He is just about to open the door and go out into the yard, when he hears a deep growl behind him. The hair on the back of his neck stands up. The inspector does not move his body but slowly turns his head.

In the darkness he can see the **shape** of Brutus. The Rottweiler is standing in the hall behind him. Brutus growls again and takes a step towards him.

"Good dog," says the inspector quietly. "Nice dog."

Although it is dark, he can see

to get a good night's sleep	durchschlafen
to swear	*hier*: fluchen
shape	Form, Umrisse
to protect	(be)schützen
to swallow	hinunter-schlucken
to tremble	zittern
to breathe	atmen

that the dog is ready to jump at him. He puts his hand in his pocket to see if he has anything to **protect** himself with. His fingers touch the bar of chocolate that he won at the fairground. Quickly, he breaks a piece from the bar and throws it to the dog. "Good dog, do you like chocolate?" he says.

In the darkness, he can see the dog take the chocolate from the floor and **swallow** it quickly. His hand is **trembling** as he throws another piece to it, and then another. While the dog is eating the chocolate, DI Rush opens the door and escapes into the yard. He quickly closes the door behind him and stands still for a moment. He **breathes** deeply and waits a few minutes until his heart is beating more slowly.

Perhaps I should have stayed in bed, he tells himself. How can I go back into the house now? Brutus will be waiting for me. If there is nothing in the barn, I will have to sleep in there until the Larkins get up. And then I will have to explain why I was out in the yard in the middle of the night.

Nevertheless, DI Rush wants to find out what goes on in the barn. In the yard there is only his car. The light is still on in the barn. He stands for a moment and listens. He can now hear noises which come from the barn. It sounds like voices – like someone talking, but very quietly.

He walks across the yard and goes to the side of the barn, where there is a window. With his hand he cleans the years of dirt from the glass until it is cleaner and he can see through it. Then, he puts his face against the window and looks into the barn.

| unconscious | bewusstlos |

At first he can only see Larkin's van. Then he sees someone moving in the corner of the barn. As they walk into the light, he gasps.

"So that's Larkin's secret," he says to himself, and he takes out his mobile phone to call the police.

At that moment, he hears a deep growl behind him. Before he can do anything, something hits him on the back of the head, and he falls to the ground unconscious.

Death Waits at the Bedroom Door

Up in her room, Sally cannot sleep. Perhaps it is the cheese that she ate at the evening meal. She wakes up several times and lies in bed listening to the owl in the wood. Then she hears a sound on the stairs.

Sally's heart begins to beat faster. She climbs out of bed and quietly opens her

several	einige

door. She sees her father going carefully down the stairs and into the hall. She does not want to speak, as she might wake the Larkins. She gently closes her door again and sits on the bed.

What should I do, she thinks to herself. What has dad seen? Should I follow him, or should I stay in my room? Finally, Sally decides to get dressed but to stay in her room and wait to see if anything happens.

Dressed in jeans and a jumper, she sits by her window and looks out onto the dark, silent yard. The night air is cool, and she is glad that she has put on a jumper.

After a few moments she hears the front door open. It is then gently closed, and she sees a figure cautiously cross the yard towards the barn. She is sure that it is her father. But what has he been doing downstairs? It has taken him a long time to leave the house. The figure goes down the side of the barn and disappears from her view.

Sally still does not know what to do. What if her father does not come back? How long should she wait before she goes to look for him?

A few moments **pass**, and she hears the sound of the front door closing again. Now she sees another figure cross the yard. Again, Sally's heart begins to beat faster. It is Mrs Larkin and she has Brutus by her side. They both cross the yard without making a sound and go down the side of the barn, where her father went only moments before.

Oh no, she thinks. What do I do now? She is feeling **frightened**, and her heart is now beating like a drum.

Exercise 8: Translation. Lesen Sie weiter und ergänzen Sie die Übersetzung der angegebenen Wörter!

DI Rush **1.** öffnet _____ his eyes and sees that he is inside the **2.** Scheune _____. He is sitting on a chair. When he tries to move, he finds that his hands are tied behind him, and his **3.** Füße _____ are tied to the chair. A piece of cloth has been pushed into his mouth. His head **4.** schmerzt _____, and for a few moments he is not **5.** sicher _____ what happened. The last thing he remembers is looking through the **6.** Fenster _____ into the barn. He looks around him. He sees again the group of men, all of them black, that he saw through the window. They look like Africans. The men are sitting around on the floor of the barn. Most of them look **7.** müde _____ and frightened. Each of them has a rucksack.

At that moment, Mr Larkin appears from behind the van. He looks across at DI Rush.

pass	*hier*: vergehen
frightened	ängstlich
murder	Mord
to plead	flehen
to fetch	abholen
to struggle	kämpfen; sich winden
wire	Draht
ankle	Fußknöchel
to get away with sth.	mit etw. davonkommen
to grab	greifen, packen

"Ah, Mr Rush. I see that you're awake," he says. "I knew that you would be a problem from the moment you arrived. Always asking questions, always looking where you shouldn't be looking. And you see what's happened. Now, I'll have to kill you."

DI Rush tries to answer, but he cannot speak because of the cloth in his mouth. Larkin comes across to him and pulls it out. The Africans watch in silence.

DI Rush breathes deeply before he speaks. "You don't have to kill me, I won't say anything. I know that you're bringing illegal immigrants into the country, but that isn't as serious as **murder**. Don't be stupid. If I disappear, my daughter will go to the police."

"Your daughter won't be able to go to the police," says Larkin in a very unfriendly tone of voice. "She will be dead as well."

"No!" **pleads** DI Rush. "Not Sally!"

"Yes," replies Larkin. "My wife has just gone to **fetch** her from her room." He begins to smile. "She's a very attractive girl, your daughter. If Mrs Larkin wasn't here, I could have some fun with her."

"You animal," growls DI Rush and **struggles** in the chair, but he cannot break the **wire** which is around his wrists and **ankles**. "You won't **get away with** this."

Larkin **grabs** the inspector's head and pushes the cloth back in his mouth.

"Oh, I think we will, Mr Rush," he replies. "This is our last job. We have been doing this for three years now. It seems that everyone wants to come to England. Most nights of the week, a group of immigrants come across by boat from France. We meet them on the beach and bring them here. We give them a drink and a sandwich and then take them to London in the van. We get one thousand

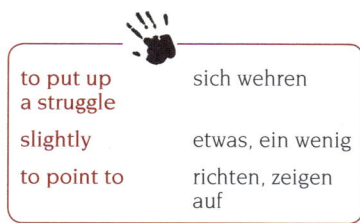

to put up a struggle	sich wehren
slightly	etwas, ein wenig
to point to	richten, zeigen auf

pounds for each one. Do you know how much money we have now, Mr Rush?"

DI Rush just stares silently at him, hate in his eyes. He knows that he cannot do anything to stop Larkin. Oh God, he thinks, I can't even warn Sally!

"Well, we have enough to start a new life in another country. Somewhere warmer than England. I don't want to work again, ever. I want to spend my time with beautiful girls." He laughs. "Don't tell Mrs Larkin, will you."

As he begins to walk away, he adds, "Well, I can't stand here talking all night. There's work to be done."

Suddenly they hear the sound of Brutus barking in the house.

"Perhaps your daughter is **putting up a struggle**," laughs Larkin. "I hope Brutus doesn't get hold of her. **i** We don't want blood all over the house."

He walks to the barn door, opens it **slightly** and looks out. Then he returns and speaks to the Africans.

to get hold of sb. bedeutet hier „jmd. zu fassen bekommen". Es kann aber auch bedeuten, „jmd. finden, jmd. erreichen": *Eventually, I get hold of Anna in Brighton.* Schließlich habe ich Anna in Brighton erreicht.

"In," he says and **points to** the back of the van. "London." The men pick up their rucksacks and begin to move towards the van. Some of them look at the inspector tied to the chair, but none of them do anything to help him. Silently, one by one, they climb into the back of the van. When they are all in, Larkin closes the doors.

witness	Zeuge, Zeugin
boot	*hier*: Kofferraum
opportunity	Gelegenheit

He looks across at the DI.

"We don't want too many **witnesses**, do we, Mr Rush?" he says. "Not that we are going to kill you here. We'll put you and your daughter in the **boot** of your car and drive it to London before we shoot you. By the time the police find you and discover who you are, we'll be out of the country. As soon as Brenda gets back with your daughter, we can go."

DI Rush tries to free himself, but the wire is tied too tightly. I will have to wait for the right moment, he thinks. Hopefully, I'll have an **opportunity** to escape when they try to put me in the car.

For the moment, however, he can only sit, watch and wait.

Exercise 9: Verb forms. Setzen Sie die Verben ins Simple Past!

1. begin _____
2. tie _____
3. shoot _____
4. look _____
5. say _____
6. do _____

7. come _____
8. push _____
9. see _____
10. have _____
11. put _____
12. know _____

Sally also sits, watches and waits. It is now several minutes since she saw Mrs Larkin and the dog disappear behind the barn. She has heard no sound, and there has been no **movement** in the yard.

She cannot decide what she should do. Should she continue to sit and wait? How long should she wait? What if her father does not come back? While she is thinking, the door of the barn opens. In the light from inside,

movement	Bewegung
cobbled	mit Kopfstein-pflaster
to reach	greifen
edge	Rand
immediately	sofort
scream	Schrei
to clatter	klappern
belt	Gürtel

Sally sees Mrs Larkin come out of the barn and close the door behind her. Brutus is by her side.

Perhaps everything is all right, thinks Sally. Dad must have heard her coming. He's probably still behind the barn.

She watches Mrs Larkin walk slowly across the **cobbled** yard and enter the house. For a few moments there is silence, and then Sally hears a sound on the stairs. She goes to her bedroom door and listens. She can hear the sound of Brutus growling quietly.

What if they have done something to dad, and now they are looking for me, she thinks. In a second, they will come in here.

She **reaches** for the key, but before she can turn it, the door begins to open. In the darkness, she sees a hand holding a pistol appear around the **edge** of the door.

Immediately, Sally throws herself against the door, closing it hard on the arm holding the gun. There is a **scream** from outside, and the pistol **clatters** to the floor. Brutus begins to bark loudly.

Sally is now able to close the door, and she pulls the chair over to hold it closed for as long as possible. She picks up the pistol and puts it into the **belt** of her jeans. She doesn't like to have it with her, but she can't leave it there for Mrs Larkin.

Now she has to escape. She knows that she could never shoot Mrs Larkin or Brutus – not even to protect her own life. I could probably overpower Mrs Larkin, she thinks, but I certainly can't fight the dog. All this flies through her mind in an instant. She runs to the open window and climbs out as Mrs Larkin begins to hit the door with something heavy. The window to her room and the window to her father's room are side by side.

to overpower	überwältigen
in an instant	in einem Augenblick
Thank goodness.	Gott sei Dank.
strength	Kraft, Stärke
prisoner	Gefangene(r)

"Thank goodness," she gasps as she sees that his window is open.

From her window she is able to climb across to his and into his room. As she stands in his room, she hears the sound of the chair break, and the door to her room opens with a crash.

"Kill, Brutus, kill!" screams Mrs Larkin and in a moment, Sally can hear Brutus barking in her room.

Quickly, she picks up the heavy lamp from the bedside table and slowly opens the bedroom door. Mrs Larkin is standing outside Sally's bedroom door and is holding her injured wrist. She is waiting to hear Sally scream when Brutus has his teeth in her.

Silently, Sally steps behind her and, with all her strength, hits her on the back of the head with the lamp. Without a sound, Mrs Larkin falls to the floor unconscious. Sally steps over her body and quickly closes the bedroom door. Brutus is now a prisoner in the room. Sally breathes deeply and now that the danger is past, she begins to tremble.

"I don't know what it is that they're doing here," she says to herself, "but if Mrs Larkin came looking for me with a gun, it must be something illegal."

Now she thinks about her father. What can have happened to him? She will have to go to the barn and see if she can find him. First, however, she must do something with Mrs Larkin.

Sally quickly checks to see if the woman is still breathing. Luckily, she is. The **blow** wasn't hard enough to kill her.

Sally grabs her by the shoulders

blow	Schlag
to drag	schleppen
to fasten	befestigen
smooth	glatt
to feel uncomfortable	sich unwohl fühlen

and **drags** her into her father's room. She uses the cable from the table lamp to tie Mrs Larkin's hands together. She then uses one of her father's belts to **fasten** the woman's legs together. Finally, she uses another belt. She puts it through Mrs Larkin's arms and fastens it around the leg of the bed.

Exercise 10: Choose the correct alternative. Lesen Sie weiter und unterstreichen Sie den richtigen Begriff!

When she is happy that Mrs Larkin **1.** can / cannot escape, she takes the pistol from her belt and looks **2.** at / on it. The **smooth**, cold metal in her hand makes **3.** her / him **feel uncomfortable**. She places it back in her belt and **4.** careful / carefully goes down the stairs. She stops at the bottom of the stairs and listens. Brutus has now stopped barking. The house is in darkness and completely **5.** silent / silence .

Sally goes to the front door and opens **6.** her / it slowly. The yard is dark and there is **7.** no / none sound. Where is Mr Larkin? **8.** Will / Should he come to the house to look for his wife? Hopefully, he is still in the barn.

Sally leaves the house and closes the door behind her. Quickly, she moves around the edge of the yard until she is at the side of the barn. She stands at the window where her father stood a short time ago and looks into the barn.

She gasps as she sees her father tied to a chair. Mr Larkin is just closing the doors at the back of the van and is speaking to her father. She can't hear what he is saying, but from the look on her father's face, it is not something pleasant.

Exercise 11: Translation quiz. Übersetzen Sie die Begriffe, um das Rätsel zu lösen!

1. überrascht _ _ _ _ ☐ _ _ _

2. klagen _ _ ☐ _ _ _ _

3. Trommel _ _ _ ☐

4. verletzen ☐ _ _ _ _ _

5. schmuddelig ☐ _ _ _ _

6. Scheune _ _ ☐ _

7. auspacken _ _ _ ☐ _ _

8. schließlich _ _ _ ☐ _ _ _ _ _

9. Pferdeschwanz _ _ _ _ ☐ _ _ _

Lösung: ☐ ☐ ☐ ☐ ☐ ☐ ☐ ☐ ☐

Larkin opens the two large barn doors before he climbs into the driver's seat of the van. As Sally watches, the van moves forward out of the barn and into the yard.

Now is my opportunity, thinks Sally.

She takes the pistol from her belt, and then she opens the

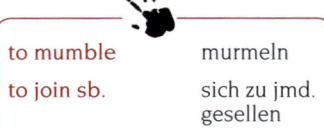

| to mumble | murmeln |
| to join sb. | sich zu jmd. gesellen |

side door of the barn. After quickly looking around, she runs across to her father with the pistol in her hand. She places the pistol on the floor and throws her arms around him.

"Oh, Dad," she gasps. "Are you okay?"

All her father can do is mumble. He still has the cloth in his mouth, so she pulls it out.

"Behind you," he gasps.

Sally turns, but it's already too late. Larkin has silently come back into the barn and before she can move, he picks up the pistol from the floor. He steps back away from her and points the pistol at her heart.

"Well, well, Miss Rush," he says. "What a pleasant surprise. So nice of you to join us."

# **Larkin Shoots**

Sally and her father look at Larkin in silence.

"Where's my wife?" asks Larkin.

"In my dad's bedroom," Sally replies. "She's unconscious, but apart from that she's okay. Oh, and I've tied her up."

"And Brutus?" asks Larkin. "I hope you haven't injured Brutus."

"No, of course not," says Sally. "He's locked in my bedroom."

"You're not just an attractive woman, are you?" continues Larkin. "I really have underestimated you. Unfortunately for you, I now

apart from	außer, abgesehen von
to underestimate	unterschätzen
body	*hier*: Leiche

have the pistol, and I won't make the same mistake twice."

"What are you going to do with us?" asks Sally.

"He's going to kill us," answers DI Rush. "The van is full of illegal immigrants from Africa. He brings them into the country every week."

"Surely it's not worth killing us to protect your illegal little business, is it?" says Sally. "In a few days every policeman in England will be looking for you."

"When they find your bodies, we will be far away," replies Larkin. "Anyway, you aren't the first to die. What do you think happened to Mr Dalton?"

"So the blood in the yard was his?" gasps Sally.

"Yes," answers Larkin. "I put him in the boot of his car before I drove it to London, so he was on the ground in the yard for a few minutes. That's where the blood came from. I didn't see it in the dark."

Exercise 12: Multiple choice. Kreuzen Sie die richtige Antwort an!

1. Where does Sally lock Brutus?
   a) ☐ in her bedroom
   b) ☐ in the kitchen
   c) ☐ in a wardrobe

2. What does Larkin plan to do with Sally and her father?
   a) ☐ He's going to drive them to London.
   b) ☐ He's going to kill them.
   c) ☐ He's going leave them in the barn.

3. Whose blood was in the yard?
   a) ☐ Mr Dalton's blood
   b) ☐ Brutus' blood
   c) ☐ DI Rush's blood

4. How much money are the Larkins paid for each immigrant?
   a) ☐ one hundred pounds
   b) ☐ two thousand pounds
   c) ☐ one thousand pounds

"But why did you kill him?" asks DI Rush.

"I can't stand around here all night talking," growls Larkin. "There's work to be done. That's your last question, Mr Rush. Dalton was our partner. He looked after the immigrants when they arrived in London. He found jobs and rooms for them. Then they had to pay him all the money that they **earned**. He was richer than we were. A few days ago, Brenda and I decided that we wanted to stop bringing in the immigrants. We're quite rich now and want to enjoy our money. Dalton wanted us to continue, but we said that we were leaving. He came here to try to **convince** us to stay. He even brought a pistol to help 'convince' us."

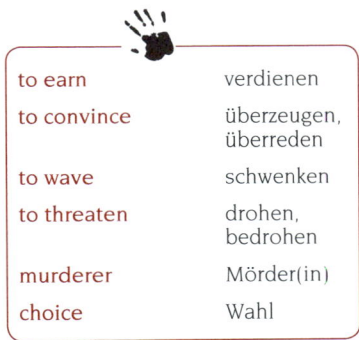

to earn	verdienen
to convince	überzeugen, überreden
to wave	schwenken
to threaten	drohen, bedrohen
murderer	Mörder(in)
choice	Wahl

Larkin laughs and **waves** the pistol around. "This pistol, in fact. When he **threatened** me with it, we struggled and I took it from him. Then I shot him. I knew he would always be a danger for us if I left him alive."

He pauses a moment and then adds, "So you see, I'm already a **murderer**. I have no **choice**. I have to kill you both."

"You won't get away with it," cries DI Rush.

"I think I will. Now, Miss Rush, please lie on the floor and put your arms behind your back. I need to tie your hands together."

Without taking his eyes from Sally, he goes to the wall of the barn and gets some wire. He returns to stand in front of her, the wire in one hand and the pistol in the other.

Sally laughs. "Do you think I'm going to make it easy for you? There are several things you don't know about me, Mr Larkin.

Firstly, I don't like someone telling me what to do. I am very stubborn. If you don't believe me, ask my dad."

Exercise 13: Unscramble the words. Lesen Sie weiter und bilden Sie Wörter aus dem Buchstabensalat!

The inspector sits there with his **1.** thumo _____ open. He cannot believe how calm his **2.** readthug _____ is. She is going to die and she is **3.** giltank _____ to Larkin as though they are discussing the weather.

Larkin points the pistol at the **4.** pinctores _____ _____.

"Either you do as I say, or your father gets the first **5.** tulbel _____," he says.

"That's the second thing you don't know about me," answers Sally. "I hate **6.** snug _____. I would like to see them all **destroyed**."

"Just be quiet and lie on the floor," replies Larkin **impatiently**. "Please let me finish," continues Sally. "As I said, I hate guns, so although I brought your wife's pistol with me, I took out all the bullets, so that no one could use it."

As she finishes speaking, she begins to walk towards Larkin. He points the pistol directly at

stubborn	stur
to destroy	kaputtmachen
impatiently	ungeduldig

her and pulls the trigger. The only sound is a metallic "click".

A look of anger appears on his face. He pulls the trigger a second time, only to hear the "click" again.

By now Sally is directly in front of him. As he swings the pistol at her head, Sally moves quickly to the side and slides her hand down his arm. This pulls him off balance. She then begins

to pull the trigger	abdrücken
to slide	gleiten (lassen)
off balance	aus dem Gleichgewicht
upright	aufrecht
to hit	*hier*: aufschlagen auf

to turn, and as she does, she takes hold of his wrist with one hand and grabs his head with the other. She pulls it against her shoulder and continues to turn.

Larkin swears. He cannot believe this is happening. He really has underestimated her. She pushes his head towards the floor, and he tries to stand up. Suddenly she is pushing him in the same direction. He is upright for only a second before he falls backwards, Sally's arm and body pushing him down. He hits the floor, and the air is knocked out of his body. Sally still holds his wrist, and now she uses his arm to turn him over, so that he is facing the floor. She picks up the wire that has fallen from his hand during the struggle and quickly uses it to tie his hands together. Then she stands up and breathes deeply.

"Are you okay, Sally?" asks the inspector.

"I'm fine, Dad," she replies. "Are you all right?"

"Apart from a bit of a headache, I've never felt better," he replies. "I always knew that I had an amazing daughter," he continues, "but until tonight, I never knew how amazing you really are. I'm so happy now that I paid for your Aikido courses."

"And I'm so happy that I took the bullets out of the pistol," replies Sally and smiles at her father.

Three days later, Sally and her father are sitting on the grass at Leeds Castle. They have just eaten a picnic of sandwiches and wine, and they both feel relaxed and happy. It is a beautiful summer evening, and thousands of other people are sitting around them. They are all waiting for the start of the open-air concert.

"There was a time when I thought we wouldn't be sitting here together tonight," says DI Rush as he puts his arm around his daughter and **hugs** her.

"Yes," agrees Sally. "When[i] Mrs Larkin came for me with the pistol and the dog, I didn't know what to do. It is a good thing that she didn't send Brutus in

to hug	umarmen
prison	Gefängnis
to suppose	annehmen
court	*hier*: Gericht
presumably	vermutlich

first. I think everything would have ended differently. Anyway, now that they are in **prison**, we can relax. I **suppose** that we'll have to come back to Kent when they appear in **court**?"

"Yes," answers her father. "That won't be for several weeks yet, though. The police have a lot of work to do before that. They told me that they have found Dalton's body in his car in London. Just as Larkin said. The pistol will have to be checked to see if it fired the bullet that killed him. They will also have to speak to all the Africans who were in the van."

Verwechseln Sie nicht **when** und **if**:
When Mrs Larkin came for me, I didn't know what to do.
(*when* = als, wenn)
If Mrs Larkin came for me, I wouldn't know what to do.
(*if* = falls, wenn)

"I really feel sorry for them," says Sally. "**Presumably** they will all be sent back to the countries that they came from?"

"I think so," replies the inspector. "But perhaps some of them will be able to stay."

44

"We are so lucky to live in this country, aren't we? And I'm especially lucky. I have such a good life here," says Sally as she hugs her father. "And I have people who love me."

"Indeed you do, Sally," says her father and smiles. "Indeed you do."

Exercise 14: Translation quiz. Übersetzen Sie die Begriffe und enträtseln Sie das Lösungswort!

1. Gefangener ☐ _ _ _ _ _ _

2. Draht _ ☐ _ _

3. bewusstlos _ _ _ _ _ ☐ _ _ _ _ _

4. gebraten _ _ _ _ ☐

5. Wahl _ _ ☐ _ _

6. ruhig _ _ ☐ _

Lösung: ☐ ☐ ☐ ☐ ☐ ☐

Death Wish

Andrew Ridley

Death on a Damp Morning

Susan Hanson stands and looks out of the house window. The rain is falling on the garden. The leaves of the trees that stand along the side of the road are wet and very green. I am so lucky to live here, Susan thinks. Bramhope is so much better than the centre of Leeds. **ⓘ** She thinks about when she was a child and the old house in a dirty street where she lived. Now she has a house with five bedrooms in one of the best areas of Leeds.

> Die Stadt **Leeds** ist das Zentrum eines Ballungsgebiets mit ca. 2,5 Mio. Einwohnern im Westen Yorkshires. Der Vorort Bramhope liegt im Nordwesten der Stadt.

But money and big houses are not really important when you are not happy. Why have five bedrooms when you do not have any children? Also, the letters which her husband **receives** make her unhappy. When she sees the postman come up to the door, Susan begins to worry. It is the same every day. Since the first letter came, she does not like seeing the postman.

to receive	bekommen, erhalten
pile	Stapel
to shake	*hier*: zittern
strange	seltsam
straight	gerade
to be right-handed	Rechtshänder sein

She goes to the door and picks up the **pile** of letters from the floor and looks through them. Her hand begins to **shake** as she sees the writing on one of the envelopes. It is **strange** writing, thin and not in **straight** lines. It looks as though someone who **is right-handed** has written with their left hand.

It is addressed, as usual, to her husband.

"Phillip," she calls, her voice full of emotion. "Phillip, there's another one of those letters."

He **swears** in the kitchen and she hears the noise as he pushes his chair back and his footsteps come down the corridor. He meets her in the **hall**, an angry look on his face. He holds out his hand and she gives the envelope to him. He looks down at the writing.

to swear	*hier*: fluchen
hall	Flur
doubt	Zweifel
drawer	Schublade
to handle	anfassen, umgehen mit
evidence	Beweismittel
to stick	kleben
to gasp	keuchen, nach Luft schnappen
chilling	abschreckend, schrecklich
frightened	verängstigt
to hate	hassen

"There's no **doubt** about it. It's the same writing as on the other two," he says angrily.

He goes back to the kitchen. Susan follows him quietly. She watches as he takes a knife from the **drawer** and cuts open the envelope. He pulls out the single sheet of white paper. He holds it carefully by one corner. Susan knows that the police have asked him to **handle** any further letters with care. They do not want to lose any forensic **evidence**.

She watches as he places the letter on the table. He uses the knife to open it out. She can see that the message has been made in the same way as the others. Someone has cut letters out of a newspaper and has **stuck** them to the paper. She **gasps** as she reads the **chilling** message on the paper.

Phillip reads the three words aloud. "You will die."

He stops and then after a few seconds he says, "Whoever sent this will be the one to die, if I get my hands on him."

"Oh, Phillip," says Susan. "I'm so **frightened**. Who can it be? Who could **hate** you so much? Why would anyone want to send these

horrible messages? It must be someone who is ill, sick in the head."

Since the first letter came, she has spent many hours thinking about it. Who could have sent it? Phillip has worked as a builder since he left school. During the past twenty years his business has grown. Now, thirty men work for him building houses. He also has an office where ten people

horrible	schrecklich
to care	sich sorgen
to upset	(ver)ärgern, aufregen
competitor	Konkurrent
victim	Opfer
several	einige
seriously	ernst
attempt	Versuch
tension	Anspannung
mood	Stimmung, Laune

work. However, the way that he has become successful has made lots of people hate him.

Phillip does not **care** about other people, thinks Susan. He is a man who only cares about himself. He does not let anyone or anything stand in his way. He never cares or worries if he **upsets** other people. Not only his **competitors** but also some of his own workers have been the **victims** of his anger and his wish to become rich. She is sure that there are **several** people in Leeds who do not like Phillip.

"Shall I ring the police?" she asks. "We should let them know that we have received another letter."

"No," replies Phillip sharply. "I'll call in on my way to the office. I want to know exactly what they have done so far. I don't think that they are really taking it **seriously**."

"I'm sure they are," answers Susan, in an **attempt** to calm him. She can hear the **tension** in his voice. She does not want him to drive off down the road in such an angry **mood**.

"I think the problem is that they don't have a lot of information to work on. It would help if you had some idea who is sending the letters."

Phillip **shrugs his shoulders** in answer. He finishes his cup of tea and then walks to the door.

"I should be home at about six o'clock," he calls back to Susan. "That is, if this **madman** doesn't kill me first," he says, and he holds the letter in the air.

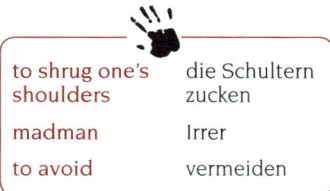

to shrug one's shoulders	die Schultern zucken
madman	Irrer
to avoid	vermeiden

Susan watches him drive off down the road. At least he has still got a sense of humour, she thinks.

Exercise 1: Translation. Wie heißt das Wort auf Deutsch? Übersetzen Sie!

1. evidence _____

2. madman _____

3. tension _____

4. attempt _____

5. victim _____

6. to stick _____

It is only two miles to Westwood Police Station but the journey takes twenty minutes. Thousands of cars are driving into Leeds and Phillip can only drive slowly. It is the same every morning, and every morning it makes him angry. He often says that he will leave home earlier in order to **avoid** all the traffic, but he does not like getting up early.

At last he arrives at the police station and finds a space to park his car. It is still raining quite heavily, so he runs to the main door of the police station.

building site	Baustelle
doorway	Türöffnung
apart from	außer, abge-sehen von

"I would like to speak to Detective Inspector Rush, please," Phillip says to the policeman behind the desk.

"I'll see if he is in, sir. Could I have your name please?" asks the policeman as he picks up the telephone on the desk.

"Tell[i] him it's Phillip Hanson," Phillip says. "And tell him that I have received another letter today. He'll understand."

Phillip stands and watches as the constable repeats his message into the telephone.

"Right," says the policeman into the telephone and hangs up.

"Would you take a seat, please, Mr Hanson. DI Rush will be with you as soon as he is free."

Phillip walks towards the seats against the wall, but does not sit down. Instead, he stands and looks out of the window into the police car park. He watches the rain as it falls onto the rows of cars. There will not be much work done on any of the **building sites** this morning.

I will be paying men to sit around, drink tea and play cards, he thinks. The sound of someone calling his name brings his thoughts back to the present. He turns and sees

> Die **Befehlsform** (Impera-tiv) entspricht im Engli-schen dem Infinitiv ohne to. Zur Verneinung wird *don't* vorangestellt: *Don't go!*

that DI Rush is standing in the **doorway** at the side of the desk.

Detective Inspector David Rush has given twenty-five years of his life to the police service. Ten years ago, his wife left him because he worked too many hours. He loves his work more than anything else in his life. **Apart from** his daughter, of course. Sally is a young woman now. He sometimes wishes that they could have spent more time together when she was young. Police work, however, has not given him much time for a private life.

He is not looking forward to his meeting with Phillip Hanson. Mr Hanson is not the kind of man that anyone looks forward to meeting, the detective thinks. He is one of those people who always seem to be unhappy and angry. It does not surprise him that Phillip Hanson is receiving **threatening letters**. The only thing the inspector finds surprising is that Mr Hanson has not received them more often.

DI Rush holds open the door for Mr Hanson.

threatening letter	Drohbrief
to complain	sich beklagen

"Good morning, Mr Hanson," he says and holds out his hand.

"There's nothing good about it," **complains** Phillip, as he shakes the detective's hand. "I've had another letter."

"Yes, I was told that," answers DI Rush, as they make their way down the corridor towards his office.

"Have you opened it?" he asks.

"Yes," replies Phillip. "It's been made in the same way as the others. The same three words

folder	Mappe, Ordner
to research	(er)forschen
to interview	befragen
forensic science laboratory	kriminal-technisches Labor
fingerprint	Fingerabdruck

as well. 'You will die,' it says. You would think that whoever is sending them would change the message a little bit."

"Yes," agrees DI Rush. "It doesn't give us much to work on. Most threatening letters are longer. That sometimes gives us a better idea of the type of person we are looking for."

They enter the office and DI Rush asks Phillip to sit down. He then opens a drawer in his desk and takes out a brown folder. He lays the folder in front of him on the desk, opens it and begins to look through the papers in it.

"Have you thought of anyone who could be sending these letters?" he asks, without looking up from the papers.

"No one apart from those people on the list I gave you last week," replies Phillip. "They're all people who don't like me. I don't think any of them would go this far, though."

"We've researched the list of names. Although you say that they all dislike you, we cannot find any evidence that one of them has sent the letters. We can't interview them without more evidence. Are there any of them who you really think could be sending the letters?" asks DI Rush.

"No," replies Mr Hanson. "I've had problems with all of them in the past, but I don't think that any of them want to kill me."

DI Rush takes a sheet of paper from the folder. He looks at it as he continues to speak. "The forensic science laboratory hasn't found anything either. The only fingerprints on the letters and envelopes are from you and your wife. The man or woman who sent them wore gloves. They have used water to wet the glue on the stamp and the envelope. Because of that there is no DNA. The only thing we can definitely say is that the letters were posted in Leeds," he adds, as he places the sheet of paper back on his desk.

"So where do we go from here?" asks Phillip angrily. "Do we just wait until someone tries to kill me? It will be a little late for me then, when I'm in the mortuary."

"We'll talk about what we can do in a moment, Mr Hanson," DI Rush answers calmly. "Do

glove	Handschuh
glue	Kleber
to post	per Post schicken, einwerfen
to add	hinzufügen
mortuary	Leichenhalle
to examine	untersuchen
impatiently	ungeduldig
to frighten	erschrecken, ängstigen
intention	Absicht
to carry out	*hier*: in die Tat umsetzen

you have the letter you received this morning? I'd like to take a look at it."

He takes out a pair of plastic gloves from a desk drawer and puts them on. He then takes the envelope that Phillip holds out to him. He examines the writing of the address, and then carefully pulls out the letter. He opens it out on the top of the papers in front of him.

"As you said, Mr Hanson, it's just like the other two," he says. "I don't think that we will find anything new here."

"So what are you going to do?" Phillip asks impatiently.

"In my experience, Mr Hanson," DI Rush begins, "people who send letters like these do so just to frighten their victims. They have no intention of carrying out their threats."

Phillip opens his mouth to say something, but the detective holds up his hand.

"Please let me finish, Mr Hanson," he says, and when Phillip relaxes again, he continues. "However, you are obviously taking these threats very seriously. Therefore, I think that it would be a good idea to put a personal alarm in your home. When you press it, it sends out a radio signal which

obviously	offensichtlich
radio signal	Funksignal
control room	Zentrale
immediately	sofort
murder case	Mordfall
sourly	griesgrämig
to pass	*hier*: vergehen
relieved	erleichtert

goes straight to the police control room. They will then immediately send a police car to your home. I will also give you an alarm to carry with you when you are away from the house. Are you happy with that?"

"I can't really ask for any more," replies Phillip, but he is not happy. "I know that you don't have enough men to give me my own bodyguard."

"That's true, Mr Hanson," agrees DI Rush. "Right, I'll send this letter off to the forensic science laboratory. You never know. We might be lucky. A fingerprint or DNA would certainly help us. And someone will phone you to arrange a time when they can come with the alarm."

He pushes back his chair as he stands up. "Unless there is anything else, I'll take you back to the reception."

"No, there's nothing else," replies Phillip. "I just hope that this does not become a murder case, with me as the victim," he adds sourly, as he turns towards the door.

Although a week has passed since the arrival of the last threatening letter, Susan still feels nervous as the post arrives each morning. She is always afraid of seeing the handwriting again. She is relieved to find that all she holds in her hand are business letters, bills and the usual **junk mail**. She carries it all through to the kitchen, where Phillip is finishing his breakfast.

"Nothing exciting this morning," she says, as she places the pile of envelopes in front of him on the table. "Can you

junk mail	(unerwünschte) Werbepost
to tidy up	aufräumen
to grunt	grunzen, grummeln
job interview	Vorstellungsgespräch
eventually	schließlich

please **tidy up** when you have finished?" she asks. "I'm going to be late if I don't go now."

Phillip **grunts** something which sounds like "Yes" and she goes to the front door. He has not wished me good luck, she thinks. She is going for her first **job interview** in over twenty years and for her it is an exciting experience.

Exercise 3: Fill in the blanks. Lesen Sie weiter und setzen Sie die Wörter an der richtigen Stelle ein!

stay work course children became looking money

For Phillip it is different. He has never wanted her to 1. _____. As soon as he had 2. _____ in the bank, he wanted her to 3. _____ at home as a housewife. They planned to have 4. _____, but it never happened. **Eventually**, she 5. _____ unhappy with her life and started 6. _____ for a job. Phillip did not want her to do that, of 7. _____.

57

"What do you need to work for?" he said, when she first told him of her plans. "I **earn** enough money for both of us."

Im britischen Englisch bedeutet **to collect someone** „jemanden abholen". Es bedeutet nicht „jemanden sammeln"!

"That doesn't matter, Phillip," she answered. She did not like to argue with him, but she felt she now had to stand up for her rights. "It's not about money. It's about me and my life. I'm lonely and bored here at home every day. I have a good education and I feel that I should use it."

But Phillip didn't give her any **encouragement**.

"**Do as you please**," he shouted and he walked away angrily.

Susan decided that she would like to work at a school. If I can't have my own children, then I'll spend my time with other people's children, she thinks. She has looked in the newspapers each week and has written to several schools.

This morning she is going for a job interview at the local junior school. They need a teaching assistant. She gets into her car and turns the key to start it, but nothing happens. Once again, she turns the key but it is the same. She does not normally have problems like this. It is, however, a **damp** morning and perhaps that is the reason why the engine will not start. Why today, she thinks. I don't want to be late for my job interview. That won't make a good **impression**.

to earn	verdienen
encouragement	Ermutigung
Do as you please.	Mach was du willst.
damp	feucht
impression	Eindruck
to slam the door	die Tür zuschlagen

She climbs out of the car, **slams the door** behind her and hurries back into the house.

"The car won't start, Phillip," she says and throws the keys onto the kitchen table.

"What do you want me to do about it?" he asks in a most unhelpful way.

He does not even look up from the newspaper as he drinks his tea and still finishes his breakfast.

"I haven't time to call the garage. May I borrow your car?" begs Susan. "You can ask one of the men to collect you [i] and take you to the office."

Exercise 4: Choose the correct verb form. Unterstreichen Sie die korrekte Verbform!

1. Susan slams / is slamming the door behind her and hurries back into the house.
2. I earn / am earning enough money for both of us.
3. Phillip has never wanting / wanted her to work.
4. Ten years ago, his wife left / was leaving him.

She does not like having to beg, but she has no choice. Even if she calls a taxi, she will still arrive late.

"Okay, if it's so important to you," Phillip replies coldly. "The keys are in my jacket pocket."

"Thanks," Susan calls over her shoulder as she runs into the hall, where his jacket is on a hook.

With his car keys in her hand, she hurries from the house a second time.

garage	hier: (Kfz-) Werkstatt
to beg	bitten, betteln
choice	Wahl
ignition	Zündung

She settles herself in the comfortable seat of Phillip's Mercedes and puts the key into the ignition.

The explosion, when she turns the key, breaks the house windows and the car becomes a ball of fire. Phillip runs from the house into the drive. At the same time, people run from the road towards the car. Phillip tries to go near the car, but he cannot because of the flames.

| to sob | schluchzen |

"No!" he screams and falls to his knees. "Susan!"

He holds his head in his hands, and his shoulders shake as he begins to sob.

He can do nothing, only watch the burning car.

Exercise 5: True or false? Kreuzen Sie die richtigen Aussagen an!

1. When Susan sees the postman, she is happy. ❏

2. Phillip uses a knife to open the envelope. ❏

3. He holds the letter carefully because it is expensive. ❏

4. Phillip encourages Susan to go to the job interview. ❏

5. DI Rush is not surprised that Phillip Hanson is receiving threatening letters. ❏

6. DI Rush thinks that Mr Hanson is not in danger. ❏

The Killer Strikes Again

"Take your time, Mr Hanson," says DI Rush. "I know that this is difficult for you, but it is important. We need every bit of information to help us catch your wife's killer."

to strike	zuschlagen
previous	vorherig, vorausgegangen
to indicate	(an)zeigen
officer	*hier*: Polizistin

He looks at the man in front of him. He does not look like the arrogant Phillip Hanson of the **previous** week. Now he is red-eyed and has not shaved. The doctor has given him something to help him to sleep, but he looks as though he has not slept for some time.

Exercise 6: Verbs. Lesen Sie weiter und unterstreichen Sie alle 14 Verben!

"If you can just tell us what happened yesterday morning. Start at the time that you got up," continues DI Rush. He **indicates** the **officer** next to him. "Sergeant Robertshaw will take notes at first. Then we will go through the story again and write everything down."

Phillip slowly begins to tell them how he and Susan got up and ate breakfast together.

There are tears in his eyes and he finds it hard to speak. Phillip tells them how happy she was about the job interview.

"I feel awful now," he says. "I just wanted her to stay at home. I didn't want people to think that my wife had to work."

DI Rush gives him a **tissue** from a box on the desk. Phillip blows his nose loudly and then continues.

"When Susan's car did not start and she asked to borrow mine, I never thought anything about it," Phillip explains to DI Rush and his colleague. "I just told her to take the keys. I was sitting in the kitchen and reading the newspaper when I heard the explosion. For a minute, I didn't move. I didn't know what it could be. I thought it was a gas explosion. As soon as I got outside and saw the car and the fire, I knew that the bomb was for me. Poor Susan died in my place. Just because her car didn't start."

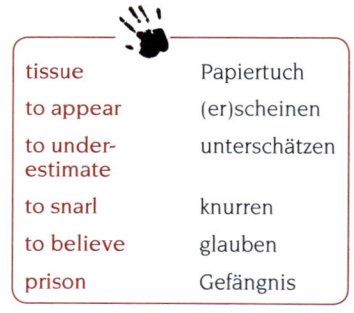

tissue	Papiertuch
to appear	(er)scheinen
to under-estimate	unterschätzen
to snarl	knurren
to believe	glauben
prison	Gefängnis

"It certainly seems that way," agrees DI Rush. "It **appears** that I **underestimated** the threats you received, Mr Hanson. Nothing like this has ever happened before."

"Yes," **snarls** Phillip angrily. "Susan would still be alive today if you were good at your job. Perhaps now you will **believe** these threats. Now that it's too late!"

"I realize that you are angry, Mr Hanson, and I understand that you think that the police could have done more. I did all that was possible with the evidence that we had," says the detective calmly.

"That may be true, but now you have to do even more," says Phillip. "I want you to catch my wife's killer. I want to see him die in **prison**."

"An incident room has been opened and we have begun the investigation already," DI Rush replies. "Detective Superintendent Whipple is leading the enquiry. However, we agree with you, Mr Hanson. We believe that the bomb was in the car to kill you and not your wife. There-

incident room	Einsatzzentrale
investigation	Ermittlung, Untersuchung
Detective Superintendent	Hauptkommissar
enquiry	Ermittlung, Untersuchung
will	*hier*: Testament

fore, we think that the killer will try again. I have to keep you alive, Mr Hanson."

"In that case, it would be a good idea if I made my will," says Phillip sarcastically.

Exercise 7: Questions about the text. Beantworten Sie die Fragen zum Text in ganzen Sätzen!

1. What did Mr Hanson think had caused the explosion at first?

   _____

2. Who is taking notes when DI Rush interviews Mr Hanson?

   _____

3. What does the police do to protect Mr Hanson?

   _____

4. Who is leading the police enquiry?

   _____

"As from now, we will **provide** a policeman who will guard you **around the clock**. He will make sure that nothing happens to you," explains DI Rush.

"Now let's go through what we know so far," says Detective Superintendent Whipple.

Around the table sit several of the detectives who are **investigating** the **murder** of Susan Hanson.

to provide	*hier*: abstellen
around the clock	rund um die Uhr
to investigate	ermitteln, untersuchen
murder	Mord
murderer	Mörder
joiner	Tischler
to go to court	vor Gericht ziehen
quarry	Steinbruch
explosives	Sprengstoff

"Would you like to start, Dave?" he says to DI Rush.

DI Rush opens the folder in front of him.

"Well, sir," he replies, as he looks at the first sheet, "it is now ten weeks since the murder, but we still do not have any idea who the **murderer** is. There are lots of people who do not like Mr Hanson. He has made several enemies. In fact, no one seems to like him. When he received the first letter, he gave me a list of all the people who might be sending them. We have checked all the people on that list. Apart from one, none of them can be the murderer. The one that we are still looking at is a **joiner** called Jack Wise. Sergeant Robertshaw, can you tell us about Jack Wise, please?"

DS Robertshaw, who is sitting at the end of the table, begins to speak. "Two years ago, Mr Wise did a large amount of work for Mr Hanson on one of his building jobs. Mr Hanson said the work was not good enough and would not pay him. Mr Wise **went to court** and in the end he got his money. However, he almost lost his business and he was very ill. There is another thing which makes Mr Wise of interest to us," continues the sergeant. "He worked at Marshall's **quarry** when he was younger. He used **explosives** there. We have interviewed him twice now. He says that he hates Mr Hanson, but that he does not want to kill him. He **claims** that

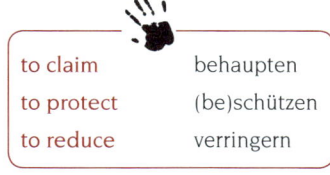

to claim	behaupten
to protect	(be)schützen
to reduce	verringern

he knows nothing about the letters. However, he was alone on the evening and night before the death of Mrs Hanson. He could have made the bomb and put it in Hanson's car."

"So, Mr Wise is the most interesting of all the people that we have spoken to so far," agrees the superintendent. "Do we know anything further about the last letter? The one Hanson received after his wife's death that said 'You will not be so lucky next time'. Could that have come from Wise?"

One of the other detectives speaks. "I'm afraid there's nothing new there, sir. We did not find any forensic evidence on the letters. As far as we can tell, each letter was posted in a different area of the city."

"At least the killer has not tried to kill Mr Hanson again," says the superintendent.

"Probably the fact that he has a policeman with him twenty-four hours each day is the reason for his good health," replies DI Rush.

"I don't know how long we can carry on, though. It is very expensive to have a detective with him every hour of the day and night. What do you think, Paul?" says the superintendent.

A thin, young detective inspector, who is sitting next to DI Rush, answers.

"As you say, sir, no one has tried to kill Mr Hanson in the past ten weeks. However, Mr Hanson complains that he cannot do his work because there is always someone with him. He wants us to **protect** him at night but not during the day. Perhaps it's a good time to **reduce** the number of hours that a detective is with him."

"Right," says the superintendent. "Well, I spoke to the Chief Constable yesterday. He wants me to cut our costs. Therefore, I am going to reduce the number of men on the enquiry next week. Unless there is some new evidence, of course. Are you going to see Mr Hanson this morning, Dave?" he asks DI Rush.

"Yes, sir. I told him that I would call to speak to him after the meeting," replies the inspector.

Chief Constable	Polizeipräsident
home-made	selbst gebaut, selbst gemacht
apparently	anscheinend
chemistry	Chemie
chance of survival	Überlebenschance
suspect	Verdächtiger
to obtain	erhalten, sich verschaffen
to join sth.	etw. beitreten
movement	Bewegung

"Could you speak to him about the protection, then?" asks the superintendent. "I think that he will be happy for us to reduce it during the day. Right," he continues, "do we know any more about the bomb?"

Another detective answers. "No, sir. The forensic report says that the bomb is home-made. Apparently, if you know a little bit about chemistry, you can easily make one. Mrs Hanson had little chance of survival. The bomb was with a can of petrol under the driver's seat."

"Okay," says the superintendent. "Sergeant Robertshaw, I would like you to concentrate on Mr Wise, as he seems to be our only real suspect at the moment. Since we are not protecting Mr Hanson during the day, I want you to watch Mr Wise during that time. If he is the killer, he may try again when he finds out that there is no longer a detective with Mr Hanson."

"Okay, sir," replies the sergeant and closes his folder. "I shall inform you as soon as we know anything."

"Please do that, Sergeant," replies the superintendent. "Right, I have nothing further to ask. Has anyone else anything to add?"

When no one speaks, he continues. "Right, gentlemen, let's get back to work. We need to catch this killer."

Exercise 8: Professions. Übersetzen Sie die Berufsbezeichnungen!

1. Briefträger _____
2. Lehrer _____
3. Baumeister _____
4. Polizist _____
5. Tischler _____

Before he leaves the police station, DI Rush discusses with DS Robertshaw how they can **obtain** more information about Jack Wise.

It is surprising what can be found out about a person these days, thinks DI Rush. When I **joined** the police, there were no computers in the police station. Now, however, we can get details of where people have used their credit card, and what they have bought with it. We can obtain their mobile phone bills. On these we can see who they call, when they call them, and where they are when they make the call. Also, cameras in the streets can record someone's **movements** minute by minute.

False friends
handy ≠ Mobiltelefon
handy = praktisch, handlich
mobile phone = Handy

With all the technology we have now, thinks DI Rush, we should be able to find out if Mr Wise is the killer or not.

He then makes his way to the offices of Hanson Construction. They are in Headingley, about one mile from the police station. When he enters the building, he sees one of the detectives from the station in the reception. As DI Rush comes in, the detective puts down the newspaper that he is reading and stands up.

"Good morning, sir," he calls happily to the inspector, a smile on his face. "How are you?"

"Very well, thank you, Colin," answers the inspector and smiles as well. "Anything to report?"

Exercise 9: Unscramble the words. Lesen Sie weiter und bilden Sie Wörter aus dem Buchstabensalat!

"No, sir. Another **1.** ituqe _____ morning. Mr Hanson is in his **2.** fefico _____. I think that the murderer knows that we are protecting him. Nothing suspicious has **3.** depapenh _____ at all."

"I have just come to speak to Mr Hanson. He wants to remove the protection **4.** grunid _____ the day. What do you think, Colin?" asks the DI.

"I don't think the **5.** redrumre _____ will strike again while we are with Mr Hanson, sir. The question is, how long can we **6.** trecopt _____ him? We can't do it for the rest of his life. It has to stop sometime," replies the detective and **7.** srghsu _____ his shoulders.

DI Rush speaks to the receptionist and then walks towards the offices. He knows his way to Mr Hanson's office. Since the murder of Mrs Hanson, he has visited almost daily. He knocks on the door.

suspicious	verdächtig
to remove	abziehen, entfernen
impolite	unhöflich
to remember	sich erinnern

"Come in, Inspector," calls Mr Hanson's voice.

The receptionist has obviously phoned him, thinks DI Rush.

Mr Hanson is seated behind his desk, which faces the door.

"Any news for me?" he asks, as the inspector enters the room.

"Good morning, Mr Hanson," answers DI Rush and thinks once again how **impolite** Hanson is. "How are you?"

"Yes, yes, I'm fine. Never mind that," says Hanson impatiently. "Do you have any news about my wife's killer? Over two months have passed since she died."

"Do you **remember** the list of names that you gave me when you received your first letter?" asks the inspector.

Hanson nods.

"One of the men on the list is very interesting to us," continues the inspector. "A man called Jack Wise."

"Jack Wise," laughs Mr Hanson. "He's not big enough to frighten anyone."

"You don't need muscles to make a bomb," replies the inspector.

"He used to work at Marshall's quarry. He used explosives there. Also, he has no alibi for the night before your wife's death. It could easily be him."

Nur als direkte Anrede oder als Teil eines Namens werden im Englischen Titel wie **Inspector** groß geschrieben.

"Perhaps you're right, Inspector," ⓘ agrees Mr Hanson. "Jack was really angry when he had to go to court to get his money. I shall never forget the hate in his eyes that day," he laughs.

"Well, from tomorrow, we shall watch him every day," says the inspector.

"He is not likely to try to kill me when I have a detective with me all the time," replies Mr Hanson.

"Well, that is the other reason for my visit today. We have decided to agree to your request. We are not going to protect you during the day."

"Good," says Mr Hanson. "You don't know how difficult it is for me. I'm trying to run a business with a detective watching me all the time."

request	Wunsch
to run a business	einen Betrieb führen
to realize	erkennen
busy	beschäftigt
to get to one's feet	aufstehen
Thank goodness	Gott sei Dank

"Of course, we realize that," agrees DI Rush. "However, your safety is more important than your business."

"Both are important to me," replies Hanson. "Anyway, is there anything else? I'm very busy."

"No," answers DI Rush, surprised once again at how impolite Hanson sometimes can be.

On his way out, the inspector speaks to the detective in the reception.

"You can come back to the station with me, Colin. Mr Hanson no longer needs protection during the day. I'm sure we can find some work that is more interesting for you."

The detective folds his newspaper. He smiles and gets to his feet.

"Thank goodness for that," he laughs. "I have read two newspapers already this morning!"

He calls goodbye to the receptionist and follows the inspector out of the door.

DI Rush buys a sandwich for lunch and then goes to see Superintendent Whipple.

"Hanson is happy for us to remove the protection during the day," says the inspector. "I have brought the detective who was with him back to the police station. He is going to work with DS Robertshaw's team."

"Good," answers the superintendent. "I was just thinking…"

crime scene	Tatort
grim	grimmig, ernst
just	*hier*: gerade eben
struggle	Kampf
to seem as though	scheinen als ob
after all	doch

At that moment, the telephone on the desk rings. The superintendent picks it up and listens for a few moments.

"Right," he says. "DI Rush and I are on our way to the crime scene now."

He puts down the telephone, a grim expression on his face.

"Well, Dave, we were certainly looking at the right suspect," he says.

"Why? What's happened?" asks the DI.

"That was the control room," the superintendent continues. "Apparently, Jack Wise has just been to Phillip Hanson's house and has attacked him with a knife. There's been a struggle and Jack Wise is dead. It seems as though Jack Wise murdered Susan Hanson after all."

DI Rush Has Doubts

When they arrive at Phillip Hanson's home, they see a uniformed police officer at the side of the road. DI Rush stops the car and speaks to him through the open window.

"What's happened?"

"Mr Hanson pressed the alarm in his house. I was the first person to **1.** leave _____," he tells them. "Mr Hanson was in the kitchen. He was holding a **cloth** to a deep knife wound to his face. He also has a cut on his **2.** foot _____. He's gone to hospital as he obviously needs to see a doctor. **3.** After _____ he left, he told me that Mr Wise came to his door. As soon as Mr Hanson **4.** closed _____ the door, Mr Wise pulled out a knife and attacked him. It looks like there was a struggle **5.** outside _____ the hall. That's where Mr Wise's **body 6.** isn't _____. Mr Hanson says that Mr Wise fell on the knife during the struggle. The

paramedics who came for Mr Hanson had a look at Mr Wise as well. They said that there was **7.** everything _____ that they could do for him. He was already **8.** alive _____."

DI Rush drives up to the house and parks the car. Both detectives go to the back door of the house where two police officers are standing.

"Have you two been into the house?" asks the superintendent.

"No, sir, we haven't," immediately answers one of them. "We are just here to protect the crime scene."

"Good," replies the superintendent. "Don't let anyone else in without my **permission**."

Followed by DI Rush, he enters the kitchen and walks through to the hall. It certainly looks as though there has been a struggle. The small telephone table lies on the floor and the telephone cable hangs from the wall. The curtains have been pulled down and pieces of a large **ornament** are lying all over the floor. There is also lots of blood on the floor and on the walls. In the centre of the hall is the body of a man. He is lying face down, a **pool** of blood near his right side.

The superintendent looks at the scene in **silence** for some minutes.

"It looks like a **slaughter-house**," he says finally. "I don't think that I have ever seen so much blood."

cloth	Tuch, Lappen
body	_hier_: Leiche
paramedic	Sanitäter
permission	Erlaubnis
ornament	Ziergegenstand
pool	_hier_: Lache
silence	Stille
slaughterhouse	Schlachthof

"No," agrees DI Rush. "It certainly seems as though the struggle lasted for some time."

Neither of them enters the hall. They do not want to **disturb** the crime scene before the arrival of the forensic team.

"Speak with the policeman outside, Dave," says the superintendent. "Tell him that only the doctor and the photographer can come in. Everyone else will have to wait until the forensic team have finished. We don't want anyone to walk on any evidence. I'm going back to the incident room. I'll

to disturb	durcheinander bringen
statement	Aussage
injured	verletzt
trial	Prozess, (Gerichts-) Verfahren
dressing	*hier*: Verband
bandage	Verband, Bandage

arrange for a team to begin enquiries at the neighbours' houses. Perhaps someone saw Mr Wise arrive."

"Okay, sir," answers DI Rush. "What about Mr Hanson? Do you want me to see him at the hospital?"

"Yes, you could do that," agrees the superintendent. "Just have a talk with him and find out what he has to say. You can take a written **statement** later at the police station. That is, if he is not too badly **injured**."

When the superintendent has left, DI Rush stands alone in the silence. He looks at the body and the blood on the floor and walls. It seems that the murder enquiry is over.

Now, all that we have to do is complete the paperwork, he thinks. It looks as though Jack Wise killed Susan Hanson and then tried to kill Phillip Hanson. There will not be a **trial**. Phillip Hanson was only protecting himself.

DI Rush arrives at the hospital as Phillip Hanson is leaving. He has a large **dressing** on the left side of his face and a **bandage** covers most of his right hand. He sees the detective in the corridor.

"Ah. The police. You are too late again, Inspector Rush," Phillip Hanson says. "It's a good thing that I can look after myself. I'm lucky to be alive!"

"Mr Hanson," replies the inspector, "we stopped guarding you during the day because you asked us to do so."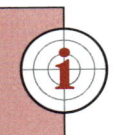

> Mit **to do so** wird hier die Wiederholung des Objekts **(stop) guarding you** vermieden.

The two men are now facing each other. The builder does not reply. He just looks at DI Rush angrily.

"I need to speak to you about the death of Mr Wise," continues DI Rush.

"Can't that wait?" replies Mr Hanson. "I'm injured. Anyway, I have already told the whole story to the policeman who came to the house."

"Well, I want to hear it from you, Mr Hanson," **insists** DI Rush. "Do you want to speak to me here, or do you want to come to the police station?"

Mr Hanson **scowls**.

"I'll speak to you here if I must," he **growls**.

DI Rush asks if he can use one of the doctors' offices. When they are both seated, he takes out a notebook and his pen.

to insist	beharren
to scowl	ein mürrisches Gesicht machen
to growl	knurren

"Right, Mr Hanson," he begins. "Could you please tell me what happened this lunchtime? I shall make a few notes while you are talking."

Mr Hanson then tells the inspector what happened. He says that he decided to go home for his lunch. He was in the house for about ten minutes when the doorbell rang.

"I opened the door. Jack Wise was standing there. I was immediately worried. You told me this morning that he was the suspect for sending the letters and killing Susan. I said to him, 'What do you want?' and he replied, 'You.' He pulled his hand out of his pocket. I saw that he was holding a large knife. He tried to slash my throat. I moved out of the way and put up my left arm to protect my face, but he was still able to cut my cheek. As you can see," he says and he points to the dressing on the left side of his face.

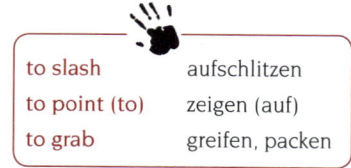

to slash	aufschlitzen
to point (to)	zeigen (auf)
to grab	greifen, packen

Exercise 11: Match-up. Welche Wörter sind Synonyme? Ordnen Sie zu!

1. ☐ wound   **a)** bandage

2. ☐ fight   **b)** grunt

3. ☐ finally   **c)** dead

4. ☐ dressing   **d)** injury

5. ☐ growl   **e)** cut

6. ☐ slash   **f)** eventually

7. ☐ lifeless   **g)** struggle

"He came after me, slashing at me. I tried to grab the knife, but it was really sharp. It cut my hand open. I have a deep cut across my hand."

He holds up his bandaged hand to show DI Rush.

"Eventually, I managed to grab his **wrist**. That's when we fell over the telephone table. He went down first with me on

| wrist | Handgelenk |
| chest | Brust |

top of him. I heard him cry out and then he was still. I got to my feet and he didn't move. I saw that the knife was in his **chest**."

He stops and thinks for a moment and then continues. "I knew that he was bitter, but I never thought that he hated me so much."

He stops again for a few moments. "Then I went into the kitchen and pressed the alarm. It was only a few minutes before the first police car arrived."

"Thank you for that, Mr Hanson," says DI Rush. "I'll leave you alone now. Obviously, I want to speak to you again and to take a written statement from you. I should just tell you that you will not be able to go home until the forensic team has examined the house. Do you have somewhere to stay for the night?"

"I can probably stay with my sister. She lives in Chapeltown," answers the builder.

"Please ring the incident room and let us know where you are," calls the inspector as Mr Hanson walks away.

Exercise 12: Verb forms. Setzen Sie die Verben ins Simple Past!

1. nod _____

2. die _____

3. think _____

4. see _____

5. tell _____

6. shut _____

7. examine _____

8. cut _____

Two days later, DI Rush is not happy.

"I know that we found one of the threatening letters in Jack Wise's pocket, sir. However, I just have a feeling that there is something not right," he explains to Superintendent Whipple. "I don't know why, but I do not believe that we have discovered the truth. Everything just seems to be a little too…"

| convenient | günstig, praktisch |
| in person | persönlich |

He pauses and tries to think of the correct word.

"I think 'convenient' is the best word to describe it, sir. The fact that Jack Wise arrived at Hanson's house only hours after I told Hanson that he was our main suspect. Also, the fact that he had one of the letters in his pocket. What do you think?"

"I have thought about it, Dave," answers the superintendent. "However, there is no evidence against Mr Hanson. I don't like him either, but that doesn't make him a murderer. As far as we know, he and his wife were happy together. Her friends say that he never threatened her. Also, he had no reason to kill her that we know of. There was no other woman in his life."

"I'm sorry, Dave," says the superintendent after a moment, "but I think that you're wrong. You will just have to accept that Jack Wise was the murderer. Look at the evidence. He had another letter in his pocket and he tried to kill Hanson. He probably came to post the letter in person, and when he found Hanson at home without a detective, he decided to attack him. I think that is enough evidence."

"Well, sir," replies DI Rush, "I just want you to know what I think."

"That's okay, Dave, but you have to accept the evidence," answers the superintendent. "Wise is the murderer. Just complete the report. There are other cases that I need you to work on."

"Okay, sir. You're the boss," replies the DI.

That lunchtime, DI Rush drives into the city centre to meet his daughter for lunch. He parks his car and walks through the streets to the café. It's a beauti-ful, sunny day and he admires the buildings around him. There are two-hundred-year-old build-ings which stand next to new

> Das **Present Progressive** schildert den Verlauf einer Handlung, die im Moment des Sprechens noch andauert.

office blocks. DI Rush really likes the mixture of old and new. It's always a pleasure for him to be in the city centre.

Sally is already sitting at a table as the inspector enters the café. She works in a bank in the centre, so they often meet here for lunch. It is the highlight of DI Rush's week. He sees her wav-ing and goes over to the table. She stands and they hug each other.

"Hiya, Dad," she says and they both smile at each other. "How has your day been?" she asks.

He does not often talk about his work, but Sally knows all about the Hanson case. It has been in the newspapers every week. It is not every day that someone in the city is killed by a bomb. She also knows about her father's feelings towards Phillip Hanson.

"I have told the superintendent what I think," replies the in-spector. "He believes that Jack Wise was the murderer. I have to agree that there is no evidence against Phillip Hanson. So now I just have to prepare the report," he says and then adds, "even though I'm not sure that Wise was the murderer."

Sally is very excited. "Well," she says, "I know something which might interest you. I shouldn't really tell you this, I suppose.

to admire	bewundern
to wave	winken
to hug	umarmen
⚡ Hiya. (How are you.)	Hallo, wie geht's.
to suppose	annehmen

It's against company rules to talk about our **customers**. Since this is a murder, though, I think I should tell you anyway."

customer	Kunde
to breathe	atmen
to suit sb.	(zu) jmd. passen
in a rush	in Eile, eilig
to insure sb.	jmd. versichern
insurance company	Versicherungsgesellschaft
account	Konto

She stops to **breathe**. DI Rush smiles. He thinks how well the name Rush **suits** her. She always speaks as though she is **in a rush**. Her words come out so fast. He often has to tell her to speak more slowly and to breathe.

"I was making a cup of tea in the kitchen at work this morning. I heard one of the managers talking about Phillip Hanson. He said that Hanson's company is having financial problems. But do you know what? The manager said that Hanson **insured** his wife for one million pounds about six months ago. The **insurance company** have told the bank that they will pay the money into his **account** in the next few weeks. I think that is a bit suspicious. What do you think?"

"A bit suspicious! I think it is very suspicious," gasps the inspector. "You are sure that's what you heard?"

"Yes, definitely," replies Sally.

"It would certainly be a good reason for Hanson to murder his wife," says the detective. "If Phillip Hanson sent the letters and put the bomb in the car himself, it explains why we didn't find any evidence at Wise's house. But if Hanson did kill his wife, why did Jack Wise attack him? That's what I can't understand."

DI Rush wants to get back to the office to look through the evidence again, but he tries to drink his coffee and eat his sandwich slowly. He talks with Sally about her work and her life. She is always such a happy girl, he thinks.

When they leave the café, Sally says, "Please don't tell anyone that I told you about Mr Hanson's account."

"No, it will be okay," DI Rush says to her. "We won't involve you, Sally."

When he arrives back at the station, DI Rush does not go to the superintendent with the new information. It's not really proof of anything. However, he thinks, one million pounds is a good reason for Hanson to kill his wife.

Exercise 13: Verb forms. Lesen Sie weiter und setzen Sie das Verb in die richtige Form!

The following week, DI Rush **1.** sit _____ in front of the computer every day. He **2.** work _____ through all the evidence that has been **3.** collect _____. As he **4.** read _____ through the report about Jack Wise, there **5.** be _____ a knock at the door of his office. DS Robertshaw puts his head around the door.

"Have you **6.** hear _____ the news?" he asks.

"Phillip Hanson **7.** sell _____ his business."

"Really?" gasps DI Rush.

"Yes," continues the sergeant. "He's leaving the country. He's going to emigrate to Brazil as soon as the enquiry finishes. I thought you would like to know, sir."

"Yes, thanks for that, Steve," replies the inspector. "Thanks very much."

to involve sb.	jmd. verwickeln in
proof	Beweis
to emigrate	auswandern

Emigrating, thinks DI Rush. He's certainly not staying around for long. After a few moments of thought, he returns to the work in front of him. He is reading Jack Wise's **medical record**. He is about to read the next document, then he suddenly realizes what he has just read. He reads it again: Four weeks before his death Jack Wise cut

medical record	Krankenakte
to dial	wählen, anrufen
to do sb. a favour	jmd. einen Gefallen tun
right away	sofort, gleich

his right arm at work. Since then he has not been able to use his right hand.

DI Rush begins to search the computer system for Phillip Hanson's statement. Yes, Phillip Hanson says in his statement that Jack Wise held the knife in his right hand. That's why the wound was on the left side of his face.

DI Rush thinks for a while. Then he picks up the phone and **dials** DS Robertshaw's number.

"Hello, Steve," he says, when DS Robertshaw answers the call. "I'd like you to **do me a favour**. Did Jack Wise have a mobile phone?"

"Yes, he had," replies DS Robertshaw. "Why?"

"Did you ever look at it to see the calls he made and received the day he died?" asks the inspector.

"No, sir," replies DS Robertshaw. "It didn't seem important at the time. The letter in his pocket and the attack on Hanson were enough proof that he was the murderer."

"Can you obtain a list of the calls that he made and received on the day he died? As soon as possible, please."

"Okay, sir," answers DS Robertshaw. "I'll do it **right away**."

DI Rush sits back in his chair with a grim smile on his face. Off to Brazil, are you, Mr Hanson? he thinks. We'll see about that!

The Last Call

"I cannot believe it, Dave," says Superintendent Whipple, as he looks up from the papers on his desk. "It looks as though you were actually right."

DI Rush tries to hide his smile of **satisfaction**.

"Yes, sir," he replies. "Not only does the **insurance policy** for one million pounds give Hanson a motive for killing his wife, but also Wise's medical record and the list of his telephone calls **suggest** that Hanson really lied to us."

"Well done, Dave," continues the superintendent. "I think we should bring Mr Hanson to the police station for an interview. He has several questions to answer."

"**Very good**, sir," replies the DI. "I'll be very happy to **arrest him**

satisfaction	Zufriedenheit, Genugtuung
insurance policy	Versicherungs- police
to suggest	nahelegen
very good	sehr wohl! *veraltet*
to arrest sb.	jmd. verhaften

and interview him. If it's okay with you, I'll take DS Robertshaw with me. He knows all the evidence as well as I do."

"Yes, do that, Dave," answers the superintendent. "And keep me informed."

"Of course I will, sir," says the DI as he leaves the office, a big smile on his face.

The first thing that DI Rush sees as they drive towards Phillip Hanson's house is the large "For Sale" sign in the garden.

"He certainly seems to be in a hurry to sell everything and leave," says DS Robertshaw.

"Yes," answers the DI. "He must be worried that we'll discover the truth."

They turn into the drive which leads to Hanson's house and park in front of the garage. Both men get out of the car. DI Rush rings the doorbell, but no one comes. He rings again and they wait for a few minutes.

Exercise 14: Unscramble the sentences. Bringen Sie die Wörter in die richtige Reihenfolge!

1. Hanson · emigrate · Brazil · Mr · to · wants · to

_____

2. police · letter · pocket · the · found · a · Wise's · in

_____

3. he · years · going · now · to · is · twenty-five · prison · for

_____

_____

4. arrest · inspector · Hanson · the · wants · to

_____

5. get · car · men · out · both · of · the

_____

"There's no one in, it seems," says the DI.

They walk around the house and look through the windows. In every room there are boxes packed with books, ornaments and other things.

"It looks as though he is almost ready to leave," remarks Sergeant Robertshaw. "At least we aren't too late."

"Perhaps he is at his office. 🛈 We'll try there," says DI Rush and they return to the car.

It's almost dark when they park the car in the car park of Hanson Construction. As they approach the building, they see Hanson lock the door and begin to walk towards his car. When he sees the two detectives, he stops.

"Inspector Rush. What are you doing here?" he asks as he tries to hide his surprise.

"Have you come to say goodbye?" he asks, laughing nervously.

"I think we need to talk before you leave, Mr Hanson," says the inspector. "I would like you to come to the police station with us."

"Sorry, Inspector. I can't do that. I have several things that I must do before I leave."

"Then, Mr Hanson, I have no choice," replies the inspector. "I am arresting you on suspicion of the murder of Susan Hanson and Jack Wise."

to remark	anmerken
to approach	sich nähern
to turn pale	blass werden, erblassen

Hanson laughs, but his face turns pale. "Is this a joke, Inspector? Jack Wise murdered my wife. I killed him to protect myself."

"It's no joke, Mr Hanson," DI Rush replies. "Now come with us, please."

"You're making a big mistake, Inspector," says Hanson.

He sounds **brave**, but DI Rush is **pleased** to see that he is **trembling** as he climbs into their car.

Phillip Hanson sits in the interview room with his **solicitor**, facing DI Rush and DS Robertshaw.

"Right," says DI Rush. "I have asked you about the one-million-pound insurance policy on your wife's life. You say, quite correctly, that it does not mean that you killed her. In your statement, you said that Jack Wise held the knife in his right

brave	mutig, tapfer
pleased	erfreut
to tremble	zittern
solicitor	Anwalt
to disappear	verschwinden
to stab	erstechen

hand. That's why the cut was on your left cheek. I have told you that Jack Wise could not have held the knife in his right hand. You now say that you were mistaken. He had the knife in his left hand. Even though he was right-handed."

"If that is all the evidence that you have, Inspector," interrupts the solicitor, "then I suggest that you allow Mr Hanson to leave."

"Yes," adds Hanson, smiling coldly. "As you know, Inspector, I have things to do before I leave the country."

"Just one more question, Mr Hanson," continues the inspector. "Can you tell me why you rang Jack Wise at two minutes past twelve on the day you killed him?"

The smile **disappears** from Hanson's face and he turns pale.

"Really, Inspector," says the solicitor. "You should have told me about this before the interview. I shall have to tell Mr Hanson not to answer the question."

"I do not think an answer is really necessary," replies the inspector. "Mr Hanson rang Jack Wise. What he said to him, I don't know, but Mr Wise came to the house. Mr Hanson knew that he was our main suspect."

DI Rush pauses and looks at Hanson. "Didn't you, Mr Hanson? I told you so that morning. When Mr Wise arrived, you invited him into the house and stabbed him. You then put the letter in his pocket. Afterwards you cut yourself, pressed the alarm and claimed that he attacked you. You thought that we would believe the story. You did not think that we would check Mr Wise's telephone, did you Mr Hanson?"

Phillip Hanson sits and stares at the table and says nothing.

Exercise 15: Translation quiz. Übersetzen Sie die Begriffe, um das Rätsel zu lösen!

1. Beweismaterial   _ □ _ _ _ _ _ _

2. Handgelenk   _ _ □ _ _

3. Brust   □ _ _ _ _

4. erstechen   _ □ _ _

5. Fingerabdruck   _ □ _ _ _ _ _ _ _ _ _

6. Versuch   _ _ _ _ _ □ _ _

7. Verdächtiger   _ _ □ _ _ _ _

Lösung: □ □ □ □ □ □ □

Six months later, DI Rush is in the café with his daughter.

"You should have seen Hanson's face when they **found him guilty**," he says. "He **denied** the murders. He said he had no idea why

to find sb. guilty	jmd. für schuldig erklären
to deny	leugnen, abstreiten
the jury	die Geschworenen
indeed	wirklich, in der Tat

his telephone number appeared on Jack Wise's telephone. Unfortunately for him, **the jury** did not believe him. He is now going to prison for twenty-five years."

"The fact that he killed his wife for money is bad enough, but to kill poor Mr Wise to give himself an alibi is really terrible," says Sally. "It's good that there are not many people like Phillip Hanson in the world."

"**Indeed** it is, Sally," replies the inspector and he smiles at his daughter. "Indeed it is."

Strangled

Alison Romer

# Strangled

Hands are around her neck, slowly pressing the life out of her body. She knows she's going to die.

She wants to scream but can't. She can't even breathe. The world turns black and there's a ringing noise in her ears.

The ringing doesn't stop.

Clea McGowan woke up with a shock. She was in her own bed. The clock on the bedside table said 4:26 a.m. Someone was ringing her doorbell.

For a moment, Clea couldn't move. She felt like a swimmer who had nearly drowned in deep water. The dream had been so real, death so close. Finally, she switched on her bedside light. Her hands went up to her neck as she looked around her bedroom.

Everything seemed normal, except for the ringing. Whoever was at her door was still there.

Clea had a sudden rush of fear. People only rang doorbells or phones so early when it was an emergency.

Something terrible has happened, she thought as she jumped out of bed. At the door, she picked up the entry phone.

to breathe	atmen
ringing noise	Klingelgeräusch
to drown	ertrinken
to switch on	anschalten
except for	außer, abgesehen von
sudden rush	plötzlicher Anfall
emergency	Notfall
to pick up	abheben (Telefon)
entry phone	Gegensprech-anlage

"Hello?" she said. She felt like she was still dreaming.

"Clea, it's us," said her mother's voice. She sounded strange.

"Mum? Dad?" Clea asked. "What are you doing here?"

"We have to come in," her father said. "Then we'll tell you."

Clea immediately pressed the buzzer and opened the door of her flat. She heard her parents come up the stairs. When they arrived, their faces were pale. Her mother immediately started to cry. Her father's eyes looked full of pain.

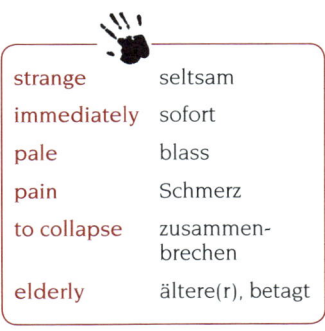

strange	seltsam
immediately	sofort
pale	blass
pain	Schmerz
to collapse	zusammen-brechen
elderly	ältere(r), betagt

"It's your sister," he said. "She's dead."

At that moment, Clea's mother collapsed. Together, Clea and her father helped the elderly woman to the sofa.

"It can't be true," said Clea. It was like she'd never woken up. It must still be a dream, she thought.

Exercise 1: Irregular verbs. Wie heißt das Simple Past der folgenden unregelmäßigen Verben?

1. ring _____
2. come _____
3. feel _____
4. find _____
5. know _____
6. leave _____
7. make _____
8. stand _____
9. tell _____
10. write _____

"She was **murdered**," said her father. His eyes filled with tears. "Our beautiful Tessa was murdered."

That night, Tessa had had a visitor. She'd **poured** two gin and tonics.[i] Both glasses were still full when the police **crime scene investigators** arrived forty minutes later.

> Achtung!
> Nicht alle englisch klingen-
> den deutschen Begriffe
> wie *Gin Tonic* sind korrek-
> tes Englisch. Richtig heißt es
> **gin and tonic.**

A neighbour had heard screaming at midnight and called the emergency number. The police found the gin and tonics, made with lemon and ice. They'd also found Tessa, **strangled** to death, lying on the sofa.

Within an hour, journalists and photographers had arrived at the house. Tessa McGowan was a well-known **news presenter**. She read the big news stories to thousands of television viewers throughout Scotland. Now her own **murder** was the big news.

to murder	ermorden
to pour	(ein)gießen
crime scene	Tatort
investigator	Ermittler
strangled	erdrosselt, er-würgt
news presenter	Nachrichten-sprecherin
murder	Mord
to answer the phone	ans Telefon gehen, abheben

Later that day, the police called Clea. They wanted to talk to her. She went on the bus to Pitt Street Police Station. The Glasgow streets looked grey and cold. Clea's head felt light, like a balloon.

She took out her mobile phone and looked at Tessa's number. They were not only sisters; they were best friends. They talked every day and told each other everything.

Now Tessa would never **answer her phone** again.

Exercise 2: Fill in the blanks. Lesen Sie weiter und setzen Sie die Begriffe richtig ein!

chairs   drunk   Everything   minutes   station

Clea got off the bus. **1.** _____ she did felt slow. It was like moving through **glue**. Inside the police **2.** _____, an **officer** showed her into a small room. It had a desk and three **3.** _____. After a few **4.** _____, he put his head around the door and asked her if she wanted coffee or tea.

"No, thank you," she said. She hadn't eaten or **5.** _____ _____ all day, but **she wasn't feeling like it** at all.

A short while later, two police officers came into the room. They both sat down.

"I'm Detective Inspector Shannon Binlow," said the woman.

Then she switched on a tape recorder. She said the time and the date.

"I'm sorry about your sister," she said in a **serious** voice.

Clea did not reply.

glue	Klebstoff
officer	*hier*: Polizist
she wasn't feeling like it	ihr war nicht danach (zumute)
serious	ernst
to go on	*hier*: fortfahren

"Now, Ms McGowan," DI Binlow **went on**, "what can you tell us about Colin MacDougal?"

"Colin MacDougal?" Clea repeated. "What has he got to do with this?"

"We've **arrested him** for murder," DI Binlow said.

Clea looked at her in shock. Colin was **married**, but he was having an affair with Tessa. It had been going on for more than a year. Clea wasn't happy about the relationship, but she would have liked Colin if things had been different. Tessa wanted him to leave his wife. He told her he would, but it was taking him a long time to do it.

to arrest sb.	jmd. verhaften
married	verheiratet
to break up with sb.	mit jmd. Schluss machen
to believe	glauben
to exclaim	ausrufen
after all	doch, letzten Endes
upset	aufgebracht, aufgeregt
witness	Zeuge

"Tessa was going to **break up with** Colin, wasn't she?" the inspector asked.

"Yes, but…" said Clea.

It was true that her sister wanted to end the relationship. The day before the murder, Tessa had called Clea.

"I can't go on like this any more," she had said. "I'm going to break up with him tonight when I see him."

DI Binlow looked serious. "That night, she told Colin it was over, and he became angry," she said. "Then he killed her."

"No, I don't **believe** it!" Clea **exclaimed**. "She called me. She was still alive when Colin went home."

At around 10:30 p.m., Tessa had called her sister again. She told Clea that she hadn't broken up with Colin **after all**. Instead, he said he would leave his wife soon. Tessa said he was stressed and **upset**, but things were okay between them when he left.

"He didn't go home," said DI Binlow. "He said he drove around in his car for another three hours. He has no alibi. He was the last person to see Tessa alive. **Witnesses** saw him going into the house at 8:30 p.m. The neighbour heard a man shouting at 10 p.m. Colin MacDougal has a motive for murder."

"What motive?" Clea asked.

"Your sister wanted him to leave his wife. She threatened to end the affair if he didn't," Binlow replied. "This made him angry. And he has a police record for violence. In 1985 Colin was arrested for fighting outside a pub. One man was hurt."

"But he must have been about eighteen years old!" said Clea. She just couldn't believe that Colin was a murderer.

"Did he ever hurt your sister?" the inspector asked.

"No!" she replied. "He loved Tessa."

"Sometimes people kill the ones they love," DI Binlow said.

When Clea got back from the station, there was a woman standing outside the door. She was holding a big bunch of flowers. It was Valerie Findlay, who had worked with Tessa at the television studio. She was a reporter.

"I was waiting for you," Valerie said. "Can I come in?"

Clea opened the door.

"I'm sorry, I'm not really in the mood for visitors," she replied.

"It's just so terrible!" Valerie exclaimed. "I can't believe it's happened!"

She gave the flowers to Clea.

"Thanks," said Clea, "but I can't invite you in. I really need to be alone right now."

"I understand," said Valerie. "If you need to talk, please come and find me. Tessa was so clever, so beautiful. She was a wonderful person..."

to threaten	drohen, bedrohen
police record	Vorstrafen-register
violence	Gewalttätigkeit
bunch	Strauβ, Bund
mood	Stimmung, Laune
closely	eng

"Sorry," Clea interrupted. "I have to go."

She went inside and shut the door, leaving Valerie on the step. As she walked up the stairs, she felt bad. The woman was only trying to help. She'd worked closely with Tessa.

Back inside her flat, Clea **realized** that she had many telephone messages. She listened to some of them: Martin McCray, who read the news with Tessa, a few old friends, a cousin in Edinburgh. There were even some from the **adult education college** where she worked. She taught **art** classes

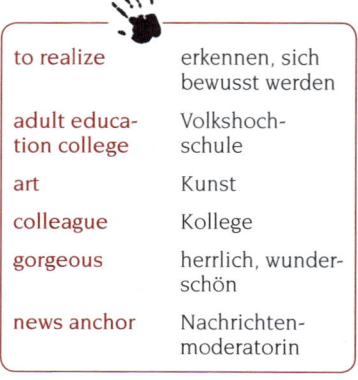

to realize	erkennen, sich bewusst werden
adult education college	Volkshochschule
art	Kunst
colleague	Kollege
gorgeous	herrlich, wunderschön
news anchor	Nachrichtenmoderatorin

there. Some of her **colleagues** had called. Everyone wanted to say how sorry they were.

She put down the phone and went to sit on the sofa. On the bookshelf was a photo of the two sisters. They'd gone on holiday to Florence together five years ago. The photo showed them smiling, with the **gorgeous** city in the background.

Exercise 3: Choose the correct alternative. Lesen Sie weiter und wählen Sie die richtige Variante!

Clea started to feel angry. Someone had **1.** taked / taken Tessa's life away. Was it Colin? The police **2.** needs / needed to make an arrest quickly. Tessa was a famous **news anchor**, so **3.** anyone / everyone was interested in the murder. It would look **4.** good / well for the police if they immediately found the killer. Clea thought about the last few weeks and about **5.** all things / everything that Tessa had said about Colin.

He wasn't exactly a 'good guy', because he had a wife and a girl-friend at the same time. But Colin as a murderer didn't seem right.

Suddenly, she **remembered** something. One week ago, the sisters had met for coffee in a café. Tessa had been happy.

"I've found a big news story!" she had exclaimed. "I've got some explosive information."

to remember	sich erinnern
to wait and see	abwarten
headquarters	Zentrale, Hauptquartier
guilty	schuldig
prison	Gefängnis
victim counselling	Opferberatung

Clea asked for more details. Tessa said she'd have to **wait and see**.

"Some people would kill for this information," she said. "I can't tell anybody yet. Not even you, Clea!"

Clea jumped up and picked up the phone. She called police **headquarters** and asked for DI Binlow. When the inspector answered, Clea told her about Tessa's information. Binlow was not really interested. The police believed that Colin MacDougal was **guilty**. That was the end of the story.

"Can I see him?" Clea asked the detective.

"You can apply for **prison** visit papers," Binlow said. "But it will take some time. I know it's hard for you to believe, but MacDougal killed your sister. Don't go to see him. It'll only upset you. Perhaps you'd like to contact our **victim counselling** service?"

Clea thanked her and hung up. She wanted to hear Colin's side of the story first. She knew that people in prison could get letters. They could send them, too.

She went to her desk and got some paper and a pen. Then she began to write.

Colin,

*I can't believe that you killed Tessa. Please tell me it wasn't you. We don't know each other, but I have a lot of reasons to **hate** you. You had an affair with my sister. You didn't care about your own wife. But I think you are **innocent** of the murder. I need to know what really happened to Tessa. Please write to me and tell me the truth!*

Clea McGowan

That afternoon, she took the letter to the prison. She hoped Colin would write back soon. Then she went to Tessa's house to start packing her sister's things. Her father and mother did not want to go. Her mother had gone to the doctor's for some tablets because she couldn't sleep. When she thought of Tessa's murder, she collapsed. She couldn't go out or switch on the TV. The newspapers and the news always had stories about the murder, and Tessa's photo was everywhere. It was hard enough

to hate	hassen
innocent	unschuldig
funeral	Beerdigung
jewellery	Schmuck
professional	*hier*: Akademiker
investigation	Ermittlung, Untersuchung
just	*hier*: gerade eben
appointment book	Terminplaner

planning the **funeral**, so Clea said she would go to Tessa's. Her parents wanted her to pack Tessa's books and **jewellery**.

The house was in Pollockshields, just outside the city centre. It was a nice, quiet area that had many large houses. **Professionals** and families lived there. Tessa's house had three bedrooms and a beautiful garden.

Inside, the police had finished their investigation, and it was as if Tessa had just left. In the bathroom, her face creams and hairbrush were still there. In the bedroom, her pyjamas were lying on the bed. It seemed that Tessa would come through the door at any minute. Together the sisters would cook spaghetti. They would have some red wine and watch a movie. Everything would be normal.

Exercise 4: Multiple choice. Kreuzen Sie die richtige Variante an!

1. Tessa has been murdered...
   a) ☐ in the TV news studio at noon.
   b) ☐ in her flat at around midnight.
   c) ☐ in a shop in the afternoon.

2. Clea thinks that Colin MacDougal...
   a) ☐ is a bad person.
   b) ☐ got angry and killed her sister.
   c) ☐ loved Tessa and is not a murderer.

3. A week before her death, Tessa had told Clea...
   a) ☐ about a big news story people would kill for.
   b) ☐ that she was marrying Colin.
   c) ☐ that she was looking for a new job.

Clea went to Tessa's desk and switched on the computer. Tessa's handbag was lying on the desk, too. Clea opened it while the computer started. There was a mobile phone, some make-up, keys and an appointment book. Clea opened the appointment book and turned to the date Tessa had died. It said: 'Colin, 8:30 p.m.'

At around 10:30 p.m., Colin had left. The police believed that he had come back again. Around midnight, there had been a **huge argument**. The neighbour had heard Tessa screaming and shouting.

Clea looked back through the appointments. She saw her own name, the day they met at the café. She kept looking back.

Then she saw a strange appointment on the 11th.

Tessa had written:

> M. 11:15 a.m., Starbucks,
> Buchanan Street.

Next to the information there was a phone number, too.

The only 'M' Clea could think of was Martin McCray. But why would Tessa meet her colleague at

huge argument	heftiger Streit
to type in	eintippen
under arrest	festgenommen
to smash	zerschlagen
to wonder	sich fragen
confused	verwirrt

Starbucks? They were together all day anyway. Tessa and Martin went to the television station at 9 a.m. in the morning. They worked hard, until 9 or 10 p.m. Sometimes they would stay even later. So who was 'M'?

Clea turned to the computer. She **typed in** Tessa's password: George.

When they were children, the family had a dog called George. Tessa had really loved him and always used his name as a password.

Clea felt guilty about looking at her sister's private papers and emails, but she wanted more information.

The police were happy to have Colin **under arrest**, but it didn't feel right to Clea. Now she had to take on the role of detective.

Exercise 5: Correct the mistakes. Lesen Sie weiter und korrigieren Sie die 6 Fehler im folgenden Absatz!

She went throu Tessa's emails. There were any from Martin, and some from an old universitie friend named Maura, both 'M' names. Clea founds Maura's number in the appointment book and called her.

Maura said she hadn't had a meeting witch Tessa on the 11th. She'd seen the news about the murder and was very shocked. Clea told her the funeral was in too days' time.

1. _____   4. _____

2. _____   5. _____

3. _____   6. _____

After they said goodbye, she went back to the emails. Suddenly she noticed some from Bonnie MacDougal, Colin's wife. It was strange that she was writing to Tessa. Clea opened one of the emails. It seemed that Bonnie knew all about the affair. Clea was shocked to read that Bonnie had threatened to come to Tessa's house and smash all the windows. In another email she wrote, "I'm watching you. I know where you live."

Clea wondered if the police had seen the messages. She thought of calling DI Binlow again. Had the police seen the threatening emails? Had they talked to Bonnie?

What if *she* killed Tessa? she thought.

There was still the question of the mysterious 'M'. Feeling confused and powerless, Clea walked around the house. She picked up some photos and books. Every time she picked something up she wanted to cry. Packing Tessa's things was too hard. It would have to wait until another day. Tessa's funeral hadn't even happened yet, and it seemed wrong to be putting things in boxes.

Just then, Clea's mobile phone rang. The number didn't look familiar. It was Martin McCray, Tessa's colleague. He started to ask how Clea was feeling, but then began to cry.

Clea was surprised. Martin was so cool and calm when he read the news. He asked Clea if she wanted to meet for coffee. She said she would meet him in a few days, then she told him about 'M'.

"Did you have an appointment with Tessa on the 11th?" she asked him.

"No," Martin replied. "And I don't know who 'M' is. Tessa never said anything about it."

familiar	bekannt, vertraut
surprised	überrascht
huge	riesig
to research	(er)forschen
to break the story	die Nachricht publik machen
career	Karriere
current affairs show	Nachrichten-magazin

"Did she tell you about her secret information?"

"She told me she had a huge news story," Martin said. "She was going to research it and break the story at prime time."

"Prime time?" Clea asked.

"That's the time when most people watch TV," Martin told her. "It's about eight o'clock in the evening."

"Did she tell you what the story was about?"

"She said it was totally secret," Martin said. "She wouldn't even tell me! A big, important story is good for the career. I think she hoped to get her own current affairs show."

"I need to know what it was," said Clea. "She said people would kill for this information, and now she's dead. She wrote a phone number down next to the name 'M', and I think I'm going to call this person."

"You should go to the police," Martin said.

"The police won't listen to me. They think her boyfriend is guilty, but I don't," she said. "There's something strange going on here and I want to find out what it is. I want to know who 'M' is."

Exercise 6: Questions about the text. Beantworten Sie folgende Fragen!

1. Who does Clea ask about the secret information?

_____

2. What did Tessa hope to get after she broke the story?

_____

3. Where does Clea find Tessa's appointment book?

_____

4. Who does Clea ring after finding it?

_____

5. Who wrote the threatening emails?

_____

2 Threatened

Clea said goodbye to Martin and put down the phone. She thought about the famous Hitchcock movie called "Dial M for Murder". Then she picked up the phone again.

She dialled and heard ringing at the other end. A man answered and said hello. He sounded nervous.

"My name is Clea McGowan," Clea said.

The man said nothing.

"Hello?" she asked. "Are you still there?"

"I'm still here," he replied finally. "What do you want?"

"I want to know if you had an appointment with my sister Tessa," Clea said. She felt nervous herself.

to dial	wählen, anrufen
to show up	auftauchen
low	*hier*: leise, gedämpft
dangerous	gefährlich

"We met on the 11th," he said. "We were going to meet again on the 15th. I waited at the café for three hours but she never showed up. Then I saw the news. I'm sorry your sister is dead. Goodbye."

"Wait!" Clea shouted down the phone. "Don't hang up!"

Suddenly the man's voice became very low. "It's dangerous for you to talk to me."

"What do you mean?" she asked. "Who are you? Did you kill my sister?"

"I think my information killed her," he said. "I believe they've arrested the wrong man."

"What is this information?" Clea asked. "I have to know. Please meet me!"

"The Starbucks on Buchanan Street, tomorrow morning at 9:30," the man said, simply. "I'll be wearing a green scarf."

scarf	Schal
unknown	unbekannt
risk	Risiko
truth	Wahrheit
jealousy	Eifersucht

Then he hung up.

Clea stood for a moment looking at the phone. Meeting this unknown man was a big risk, but she had to know the truth.

She made a quick call to Martin. He didn't answer his phone, so she left a message about meeting 'M'. Then she put on her coat and hat. She picked up Tessa's appointment book and found Colin's address. There were many motives for murder, and Bonnie MacDougal had one of them: jealousy. If Clea was now a detective, she had to get as many facts as possible.

A short time later, she arrived outside the MacDougal house. She was shocked to see news reporters and cameramen outside. They took some photos of her and one even called out her name. They knew she was Tessa's sister. She didn't speak to them.

At the front door she rang the doorbell. A short, thin woman answered it, but only opened the door enough to put her head around it.

"What do you want?" she asked. "I don't talk to reporters."

"I'm Tessa's sister," Clea replied.

"Go away!" Bonnie suddenly shouted.

She tried to close the door, but Clea put out her foot and held the door open. She heard cameras taking pictures, and wondered how it would be reported in the news the next day.

"Let me in, or I'll tell these news reporters about the emails," Clea said quietly.

She didn't really want to do that, but she had to get inside some-how.

to confess	gestehen
behaviour	Verhalten

Finally, Bonnie let Clea in. Before Clea could speak, Bonnie turned around and started to cry.

"I know he didn't kill your sister," she said. "I am one hundred per cent sure he didn't kill her!"

Exercise 7: Synonyms. Lesen Sie weiter und ergänzen Sie die passenden Synonyme!

"I think Colin is **1. not guilty** _____, too," said Clea, sitting down on the sofa. "The real **2. killer** _____ is out there somewhere. **3. Maybe** _____ he, or she, feels guilty that an innocent man is in **4. jail** _____. If the **5. true** _____ killer **confessed**, Colin would be freed."

She looked at Bonnie seriously.

"What are you **6. telling me** _____?" Bonnie said. "Do you think I did it?"

"You wrote threatening emails to Tessa. The police would prob-ably be very interested in those emails."

"I was very angry when I wrote those emails," Bonnie said. "I was so jealous. Colin stayed out late. His **behaviour** changed. I wanted to hurt your sister, and I hated her. But I didn't kill her!"

Clea stood up.

"Maybe you did," she said. "Maybe you followed Colin to Tessa's house that night. You hear them have an argument. You see Colin leave. You wait a bit, and then ring Tessa's bell. She lets you in because she can see you're upset. She makes

⚡ hen party	Junggesellin-nenabschied
to yell	schreien, rufen
to set off	sich auf den Weg machen, aufbre-chen
strength	Stärke, Kraft
revenge	Rache

some drinks and tries to talk with you. But you threaten her, you shout at her, then you strangle her."

"No!" Bonnie exclaimed. "I didn't do it! I was away that night. My friend was getting married and we had a hen party in Edinburgh. I have an alibi!"

"You have an excellent motive for murder! Were you jealous enough to kill my sister?" Clea exclaimed.

"Get out of my house now!" Bonnie yelled. "I'll call the police if you don't go!"

Clea didn't say another word. She went to the front door. As soon as she opened it, she heard cameras. The reporters started shouting. Bonnie shut the door with a loud bang, and Clea set off towards the bus stop.

The reporters followed her for a while, asking questions. When she didn't answer, they gave up.

As Clea got on the bus, she thought about Bonnie. She was a small, thin woman, but anger gave people extra strength. She could have strangled Tessa. Tessa was dead and Colin was in prison. Bonnie had perhaps taken revenge on the two people who had hurt her.

However, there was the hen party. That was a problem. Maybe Bonnie had five or six alibis, or maybe she didn't.

Clea decided she would write to Colin again and ask him for the names of Bonnie's friends. Then she would visit the friends, even if she had to use Tessa's car and drive to Edinburgh. The women would remember Bonnie at the party. That is, if Bonnie was telling the truth. At the same time, she felt sorry for Bonnie. She had lost her husband first to Tessa, and then to prison.

After getting off the bus, she walked up her street. Someone was standing at the door of the house.

It was Valerie Findlay again.

Clea was not happy to see her. Of course Valerie cared, but Clea just wanted to be alone. Although she was a colleague, Tessa hadn't really liked the woman. They saw each other at parties, but they were never friends, unlike Tessa and Martin.

to care	sich sorgen, betroffen sein
unlike	anders als, im Unterschied zu
to unlock	aufschließen
brave	mutig, tapfer
with all one's heart	von ganzem Herzen
over and over	immer wieder

"Hello, Valerie," said Clea.

"I'm very worried about you!" Valerie said. "I spoke to Martin. He told me all about the mysterious man Tessa was meeting for information."

Clea unlocked the door. Together the women went up the stairs to the flat. Once inside, Valerie took off her coat.

"Meeting this man alone is too dangerous," she said. "I think someone should go with you."

"I'm fine on my own," Clea replied. "We're meeting at Buchanan Street Starbucks. There'll be lots of people around."

"It's not a game, Clea!" Valerie exclaimed. "You're not really a detective. I think Colin MacDougal is the murderer, but maybe it was someone else. You can't be sure. I'm going to come with you. He can't hurt you if there are two of us."

Clea didn't want Valerie to come, but she was right: it might be dangerous. It was better to have a witness.

"Okay," she said. "We'll go together. But I want to talk to 'M' alone first. He might be angry that I've brought someone else, but I'll get him to talk to us both."

Exercise 8: Match up the phrases. Was gehört zusammen? Verbinden Sie!

1. ☐ tell   **a)** an argument
2. ☐ send   **b)** a scarf
3. ☐ watch   **c)** a question
4. ☐ have   **d)** the truth
5. ☐ wear   **e)** the news
6. ☐ ask   **f)** an email

The next morning Clea had a quick breakfast. The post arrived and there was a letter from Colin. As she read it, Clea felt like crying.

Dear Clea,

I am so sorry for hurting your sister. She wanted me to leave my wife, but I wasn't **brave** enough to. However, I loved Tessa **with all my heart**. We had an argument that night; but I didn't kill her and that's the truth. I cry every night because she's gone. I tell them **over and over** I didn't do it. I didn't go home for a long time because I was upset and I didn't know what to do. I should have left my wife a long time ago. If I had, Tessa would still be alive. I decided to leave my wife the next day, but now it's too late and Tessa will never know how much I loved her.

Please believe me, Clea, I didn't do it!

Colin

Clea believed him. She'd been unhappy about the affair. Sometimes she had been angry with Colin, and with Tessa, too. However, Colin wasn't a bad man; he'd just done the wrong thing. Now Clea had to find out who really killed Tessa. If the police wouldn't start a new investigation, Clea would have to do so alone.

Exercise 9: True or false? Kreuzen Sie die richtigen Aussagen an!

1. Clea takes her car to visit Bonnie MacDougal. ❐

2. At first, Bonnie MacDougal thinks that Clea is a reporter. ❐

3. Bonnie is a tall and thin woman. ❐

4. Martin tells Valerie Findlay about Clea's plan. ❐

5. Tessa and Valerie were close friends. ❐

6. The unknown man will be wearing a green scarf to meet Clea. ❐

3 Scared

At 9:25 Valerie and Clea met at Starbucks. Valerie sat at another table. She agreed that Clea would go up to the man alone, and explain that she'd brought someone else. Then they would talk to 'M' together.

Clea looked around. Right at the back of the café she saw a man with a green scarf. He had a brown jacket, dark brown hair, and was wearing glasses. He looked about thirty-five years old. He also seemed nervous.

to go up to sb.	auf jmd. zugehen
to be at stake	auf dem Spiel stehen
scientist	Wissenschaftler
it's my fault	es ist meine Schuld

Clea went up to him and introduced herself. Then she sat down. "I need to know why my sister died," she said. She didn't want to make small talk. "How dangerous is this information really?"

"There's a lot of money at stake," the man replied. He didn't want small talk either. "Hundreds of millions, maybe even billions of pounds. That kind of money can make people kill."

"Who are you?" Clea asked.

"My name is Marcus," said the man. "I'm a scientist."

Clea looked surprised. A scientist?

"What do you know about Tessa's murder?" she asked.

"I feel it's my fault," Marcus replied. "I contacted Miss McGowan because I needed to tell somebody about all of this. I'm just a scientist, but your sister knew all about news and information. I needed help and thought she was the right one to help me.

I knew the information was dangerous. Now she's dead. So I'm guilty of her murder."

"But *you* didn't kill her," Clea said. "Look, you need to tell me the whole story. I've brought someone with me who can help, too."

"What?" Marcus yelled.

He stood up. "I wanted you to come alone! I think they're watching me. It's very dangerous."

to end up	(schließlich) enden, landen
to recognize	(wieder)erkennen
to join sb.	sich zu jmd. gesellen
to put out one's hand	die Hand ausstrecken
frightened	verängstigt

"Calm down," Clea said. "Valerie is a reporter. She was a colleague of Tessa's."

"If they see me with a reporter, I could **end up** dead," said Marcus, sitting down again. "So could you."

"Who are you talking about?" asked Clea. "Who are 'they'?"

She was starting to get worried. She looked around the room.

Perhaps someone was watching them all the time. Alone, she and Marcus could be two friends, but Valerie was on TV. Everyone would **recognize** her.

"If you think this reporter can help, I'll talk to her," said Marcus. "But you're both taking a risk ⓘ by speaking to me."

Clea looked over to Valerie and made a sign for her to **join them**. She came over and **put out her hand** for Marcus to shake. Then the three of them sat down together. Valerie had a cup of coffee with her, but Clea was too nervous to drink anything. She wondered how Valerie could be so calm.

Marcus told them that he wanted to go to the police, but was too **frightened**.

Wie hier drückt **to take** in vielen Wendungen aus, dass eine Handlung bewusst erfolgt:

| **to take a risk** | ein Risiko eingehen |
| **to take a chance** | die Chance ergreifen |

"The police might not be interested," he said. "Then my life will be in danger because they'll know I went to the police."

"Please tell us everything," said Clea.

"Right from the beginning," Valerie added. "Then we can decide what to do."

Marcus opened his leather bag and pulled out some documents in a file. Then he told them about his job as a scientist. A large multi-national company wanted to build a processing plant just outside Glasgow. The area was famous for its beauty and had lots of

to add	hinzufügen
leather	Leder
file	Akte
company	Unternehmen
processing plant	Verarbeitungs- anlage
plant	Pflanze
ecosystem	Ökosystem

different kinds of plants and animals. A processing plant might threaten the ecosystem, so scientists had to study the area first.

The research would show if it was safe to build the processing plant. After the research was finished, the government had the power to say 'yes' or 'no' to the company. The company paid a team of scientists to study the area, and Marcus was one of them.

"These documents show the results of the research," Marcus said, holding up the file. "They were given to the govern-ment.

research	Forschung
government	Regierung
to run the company	das Unternehmen leiten
false	falsch, gefälscht
certain kinds	bestimmte Sorten
environment	Umwelt
to be involved	beteiligt sein, verwickelt sein

The results are good. The environment won't be threatened and the processing plant will be built. The men who run the company will make millions of pounds, and there'll be new jobs in the area."

"So what's the problem?" Clea asked. "Why are the documents so dangerous?"

Marcus answered very quietly.

"The results are false," he said. "The company is paying some of the scientists in more ways than one. They're paid to do the research, and then they're paid extra money to make the results false. I found out. I also have other documents which show the real results of the research. Certain kinds of plants that are important to the ecosystem will be threatened. It's too dangerous to build the processing plant there. It would be very bad for the environment."

"That's terrible!" Clea exclaimed. "How could anyone do that?"

"It's about money," Marcus replied. "I think someone in the government is involved, too. Perhaps the company is paying him to help."

"So you contacted Tessa," said Clea. "You wanted her to break the story."

"Yes," Marcus said. "I thought everybody should know. I needed the help of a journalist. Tessa

to hire	anheuern, beauftragen
luxury	Luxus, luxuriös
straight away	direkt, sofort
official	Beamter, Offizieller

was famous and important, so people would listen to her. Tessa and I planned to hire a private detective to follow the men from the company. We wanted to follow the scientists and the government officer, too. We needed to get as much extra information as possible. The truth is, lots of people could end up in prison.

Exercise 11: Opposites. Lesen Sie weiter und ergänzen Sie das Gegenteil der angegebenen Begriffe!

That's why the information is so 1. safe _____.

There's one big boss of the company and he could 2. start _____ up in prison himself. He'd 3. win _____ his luxury lifestyle. It could threaten the whole company 4. nationally _____. Think of 5. none of _____ the money!"

"Why didn't you 6. come _____ to the police straight away?" 7. answered _____ Clea.

"I thought that a government official was involved. Also, the company boss, Mr Wester, is a multi-millionaire. All that

115

power and money can make documents and even people **disappear**."

"Did you give some documents to Tessa?" Clea asked.

"She had copies, yes," Marcus replied.

to disappear	verschwinden
to imagine	sich vorstellen
meanwhile	währenddessen
to make sth. public	etw. publik machen, etw. veröffentlichen

"I didn't see them in her desk. I wonder where they could be."

Clea thought for a moment about Tessa's murder. She **imagined** the scene.

A man phones Tessa that night and says he has information about the research. He says he's a scientist, someone who knows the real results. Like Marcus. At home, Tessa waits for Colin. He arrives and they argue. At around 10:30 p.m. he leaves and drives round and round the streets. He doesn't want to end the affair, but he doesn't want to upset his wife. **Meanwhile**, Tessa's next visitor arrives. The false scientist. She's happy to see him because he has more information. But he doesn't help her. Instead, he strangles her to death.

"What if Tessa told the murderer that you had documents and wanted to **make them public**?" Clea asked Marcus.

"Maybe she didn't have to," he replied. "Maybe they already knew about me and I led them to her. It would have been easy for them to follow me when I met her here the first time. But I don't really understand why I'm still alive. Every time I go out, or the doorbell rings, I think that my life is over."

"There's only one thing to do," Clea said.

"Yes!" Valerie exclaimed. "You must give the information to me."

"No!" Clea and Marcus said at the same time.

"I'll hire a private detective myself, then break the news story," Valerie said, putting her hand on the documents.

"Tessa was murdered!" Clea said angrily. "Perhaps it was because of this information. Tessa should have gone to the police, and now we have to, Valerie."

"Absolutely," said Marcus. "We'll be safer if we go together. The three of us can't be killed all at once."

absolutely	*hier*: ganz genau
all at once	alle gleichzeitig
offer	Angebot

"The murderer has been found," Valerie said. "Colin MacDougal did it! The information won't kill me, and I need you to give it to me now!"

Clea and Marcus looked at each other. Slowly, Clea shook her head.

"You can't be sure, Valerie," she said.

Suddenly Valerie jumped up out of her chair.

"You will not go to the police!" she shouted. "Someone else will get the story then, and my chance will be gone!"

Everyone in the café looked at her. She sat down again and spoke in a low voice.

"I deserve it! I should have been news anchor already, not Tessa. Now the station needs a new one, and that's going to be me! I'm not going to do boring reports about festivals and lost dogs any more. This information will make my career, [i] so don't stand in my way!"

She quickly picked up the documents from the table, then stood up and ran out of the café.

Clea was shocked. Valerie had used her to get the information. Her offer of help hadn't been real. She couldn't move for a moment, but then jumped up

Die Wendung **make my career** kann man übersetzen mit „meine Karriere zum Erfolg führen" oder auch „mich berühmt machen".

and ran out after Valerie. She saw Valerie run along the street until she found a taxi; then she got into it and drove away. Clea was left standing on the street alone.

A minute later, Marcus came up behind her.

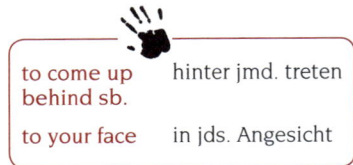

to come up behind sb.	hinter jmd. treten
to your face	in jds. Angesicht

"She only has copies of the documents," he said. "I have the original ones at home."

"We should go to the police together," Clea said. "Valerie's life could be in danger."

She felt like crying. Valerie's bitter words had upset her, and she remembered what Tessa had said about her colleague.

"She can smile and be sweet to your face. But then, when she turns away, her smile disappears."

Marcus put his hand on Clea's arm.

"Let's go to the police immediately," he said.

Exercise 12: Present Continuous. Setzen Sie die Verben ins Present Continuous, um zu zeigen, dass in diesem Moment eine Handlung vollzogen wird!

1. Clea and Marcus meet _____ in the café.

2. She catch _____ a taxi on the street.

3. I think _____ of going to the police.

4. We wait _____ outside the building.

5. He hit _____ the ball against the wall.

Hunted

At Pitt Street Police Station, they asked for Detective Inspector Binlow. She didn't look happy to see Clea again.

"A witness saw Colin MacDougal's car near Tessa's house at 11:15 p.m.," Inspector Binlow said. "Have you come to tell me he's innocent? If so, you're **wasting** your time."

hunted	gejagt
to waste	verschwenden
curious	neugierig
to deal with sth.	sich kümmern um
crime	Verbrechen

Marcus stepped forward. He told[i] Binlow all about the false research results. He told her how Tessa had become involved.

Then together he and Clea explained that Valerie Findlay had run off with the information.

The DI was **curious**.

"This company has done something totally illegal," she said, [i] "and we have special officers who **deal with** this kind of **crime**. I'll call them right now. Can you stay here until they've talked to you?"

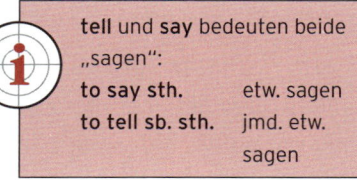

tell und **say** bedeuten beide „sagen":
to say sth.   etw. sagen
to tell sb. sth.   jmd. etw. sagen

Clea and Marcus were glad someone was listening to them. Binlow had realized how serious it was, although she still didn't believe it had anything to do with the murder.

"One more thing, Ms McGowan," said Binlow before she left. "You seem to be playing private detective. It's a bad idea. Leave the investigations to the police. That's our job."

Clea said nothing. She was happy that Binlow was taking them seriously, and that an investigation would start. But until the real murderer was arrested, she would keep searching for clues.

Clea and Marcus waited for half an hour. Finally, two other officers came into the room. They wanted to hear the story, and needed to see the original documents. One of them said he would go home with Marcus and get them. Clea was free to go, but Marcus was worried. He wanted a police officer to go with Clea, too.

"Her life could be in danger!" he said.

"We don't know that," said the officer. "But if it makes you feel

to keep doing sth.	weitermachen mit
clue	Hinweis, Spur
to be free to…	jmd. freistehen zu …
genuine	wirklich, echt
protection	Schutz, Bewachung
busy	beschäftigt
to trust sb.	jmd. vertrauen

better, we'll drive by Miss McGowan's house every hour tonight. But until we know you are in genuine danger; we can't give you an officer for full-time protection. We're really busy trying to deal with all the crime in this city. I'm sorry, that's just the way it is."

Marcus wrote down his address and phone number and gave them to Clea.

"Please call me every few hours," he said. "I want to know you're okay. If you're frightened or need any help, just call or come over to the flat. I'm not very brave, but I don't want anything to happen to you."

"Thanks," said Clea. "Here's my address and phone number, too. I'm not very brave either, but I can call the police!"

Exercise 13: Unscramble the words. Lesen Sie weiter und und bilden Sie Wörter aus dem Buchstabensalat!

Clea caught a bus home. She thought **1.** otabu _____

Marcus. Already he felt like a **2.** endirf _____.

The fact was, however, she knew **3.** hington _____

about him. Was he telling the **4.** hturt _____?

The research **5.** ocudstmen _____

looked real, but it would be easy to make those. All you

needed was a **6.** retpumoc _____.

Now she'd given him her address and phone number. He seemed nice and she felt she could trust him. But perhaps she was wrong. Now, for some reason, she felt nervous about going home.

At the next stop, near the George the Fifth Bridge, she got off the bus. She took out her mobile phone and Tessa's appointment book, found Valerie's number and dialled it. There was no answer. The police said they would contact Valerie immediately. Maybe she was with them right now. Clea just had to hope for the best. She thought about Marcus again. His flat was near Pitt Street Police Station, so it wouldn't take him long to give the documents to the officer. Then what would he do? Would he be safe at home? Could she trust him? Marcus said the scientists were paid a lot of extra money for giving false research results. Was it enough money to kill for? Clea had so many questions and no answers.

She walked along the bridge and looked down at the River Clyde. ⓘ In wintertime there was always a lot of water, and the river was flowing very fast. She stopped on the bridge and looked over.

She thought about the times she and Tessa had walked through Glasgow city centre. They had shopped, and gone to cafés and art galleries. Tessa had loved the artist Rennie Mackintosh, so they often went to the café at the Mackintosh Gallery. Now Clea was alone. Her sister and best friend was dead.

Suddenly, she heard a loud noise behind her. It sounded like car tyres. She looked around and was shocked to see a dark car with dark windows had driven right off the street. It was driving up onto the pedestrian walkway and was heading straight for Clea. She was alone on the bridge, and there was nowhere for her to run.

Clea got up onto the side of the bridge and jumped. She heard the car crash into the side of the bridge. Then the tyres made a screaming noise as the car pulled away again.

Suddenly she was under water. The cold was a huge shock. She'd hit the water very hard, so for a moment she was confused and her head hurt. She couldn't breathe.

I'm going to drown! she thought.

It took a lot of effort to move her arms and legs, but finally she managed to swim upwards towards the air. She managed to get her head above water and take a few deep breaths. Water

to flow	fließen
tyre	Reifen
pedestrian walkway	Bürgersteig
to head straight for	direkt zusteuern auf
to hit	*hier*: aufschlagen auf
effort	Anstrengung, Einsatz

was in her mouth and nose, and she was almost crying.

The river flowed so fast it simply **pulled her along**. She couldn't swim against it. The **riverbank rushed past** on both sides. She tried to swim towards it, but she wasn't strong enough to fight the water.

to pull sb. along	*hier*: jmd. mitreißen
riverbank	Flussufer
to rush past	schnell vorbei-ziehen
to wave	winken, schwenken

Just then, she saw two people, a man and a woman. They were slowly walking along the riverbank. When they saw Clea, they started to shout and **wave** their arms. But the river was too fast. Clea saw the woman take out her mobile phone. Then they were too far away for her to see any more.

Exercise 14: Odd one out. Welches Wort passt nicht in die Reihe? Unterstreichen Sie das „schwarze Schaf"!

1. witness   policeman   crime   victim
2. scream   whisper   yell   shout
3. choke   drown   wave   strangle
4. effort   result   memory   properly
5. unskilled   clever   smart   intelligent
6. help   worry   assist   aid

Buildings went past quickly on each side. The water was cold, too cold. Clea could feel the energy disappearing from her body, and the water was pulling her under again. It suddenly seemed easier to simply give up, stop fighting, and go under. Then she thought of her parents. One daughter murdered, the other drowned. They would never get over it. She had to make one last effort!

There were trees and bushes along the riverbank. Using all her strength, Clea tried to swim towards them. She got a little bit closer, and closer still. The current wasn't as strong towards the edge of the river. It was getting easier to swim. Finally she could reach out her hand towards some bushes that were low down, close to the water. They had no leaves, but they were strong.

current	Strömung
to reach out	greifen nach
burst of energy	Energieschub
mud	Schlamm
freezing cold	eiskalt
properly	richtig
she felt sick	ihr war übel
relieved	erleichtert
to pull over	*hier*: an den Straßenrand fahren
to shake	zittern

With a final burst of energy, she pulled herself up out of the water, then fell into the mud of the riverbank. She turned onto her back, breathing quickly. All her energy was gone and she was freezing cold. Her bag was still across her body. She slowly sat up and opened the bag.

Everything inside was totally wet. Her mobile phone had stopped working. She looked around, but there were no people. There was a street not far away. She managed to stand up, but her legs were not working properly. It wasn't easy to walk and she felt sick.

On the street a few cars drove past. The drivers saw her but didn't stop. After a few minutes, a truck came along, and Clea was relieved to see the driver pull over at the side of the road. He opened the door.

"What happened to you?" he asked, starting to laugh. Then he looked at Clea's face.

"I fell into the river," she said.

Her clothes and hair were wet. She was shaking with shock and cold.

"You don't want to go swimming in the Clyde in winter," said the truck driver. "It's too cold. Summer is better. Do you need a ride?"

Clea said yes, and got into the truck. She knew she should tell

You don't want to…	Du solltest nicht …
Do you need a ride?	Soll ich dich mitnehmen?
memory	Erinnerung
to choke	ersticken

the police immediately that somebody had tried to kill her. All she could think about, however, was getting home. She wanted a hot shower and dry clothes.

The truck driver took her right to her front door. Clea thanked him.

"Will you be okay?" he asked.

"I think so," she replied. "I just need to get warm."

She went inside. After showering, she put on some clean, warm pyjamas ⓘ and went into the living room. She was still shaking badly. She opened her bag and took out the paper with Marcus's number on it. It was wet, but she could just read the numbers.

She dialled his home, but there was no answer. Then she tried his mobile, but all she got was his voicemail. She didn't leave a message.

"Where is he?" she said out loud. Then she called the police and asked for DI Shannon Binlow. The

> **pyjamas** (Schlafanzug) ist ein sogenanntes Paarwort, das keine Singularform besitzt. Mengen werden bei diesen Substantiven mit **a pair of** angegeben:
> *She bought two pairs of pyjamas.*

detective asked her a few questions, but Clea couldn't offer much help. The car had been dark, with dark windows. She hadn't seen the driver and didn't even know what kind of car it was. Her memories were mainly of being in the water, choking, not able to breathe.

Binlow said she would come to the house right away and told Clea to lock the door until she arrived.

"I'm starting to think you could be right," Binlow said. "Maybe MacDougal is innocent after all. Switch on your TV."

Exercise 15: Plurals. Geben Sie die Pluralform an!

1. plant   _____

2. woman   _____

3. story   _____

4. information   _____

5. colleague   _____

6. gin and tonic   _____

7. piece   _____

8. bush   _____

Clea put down the phone and switched on her television. The news had just started. Martin, Tessa's colleague, was reading it. The picture showed the police arresting a businessman who was wearing an expensive suit. They were taking him to a waiting

right away	sofort, gleich
landscape	Landschaft

police car. Martin said that the man was Mr Charles Wester. Marcus had talked about Wester that morning! She turned up the sound on the TV.

The report said that Wester paid scientists for false research results. Then the picture changed to show a beautiful landscape.

There were many tiny plants and animals that played an important role in the ecosystem of the area. Martin explained that two other company managers, a government officer and three scientists were also being questioned.

"There may be a connection with the murder of my friend and colleague, Tessa McGowan," Martin said. "Police have started an investigation. This could be good news for Colin MacDougal, who is under arrest for the murder."

Clea felt she could breathe again. Maybe the real killer would be found and Colin would be free. She was about to try calling Marcus again when the doorbell rang. She went to the entry phone and picked it up.

"Hello?" she said. She hoped it was either the police or Marcus. Instead, it was Valerie.

"Clea, you have to let me in. It's very important," she said.

"I don't want to talk to you," Clea said. "You used me to get that information. You only thought about your career."

tiny	winzig
to be ques-tioned	verhört werden
connection	Verbindung
What's the matter?	Was ist los?

"I'm sorry," said Valerie. "Look, I was wrong to behave that way. But now I really need to see you. Let me in."

"You can come in for a minute," Clea said. "But I'm still very angry."

She pressed the buzzer and opened the door of her flat. She heard Valerie come up. When she reached the top of the stairs, Clea was shocked to see her face. The woman looked pale.

"What's the matter?" Clea asked.

Valerie came through the door and didn't even close it behind her before she started shouting.

"You gave those documents to the police!" she exclaimed.

"Yes, we thought…" Clea started to say.

"I told you not to!" Valerie said. "That was my story!"

"Please don't be so upset, Valerie," said Clea. "I need to know who killed my sister. Maybe an innocent man is in prison."

"I don't care about him!" Valerie yelled. "That information would have made my career!"

She reached over to the coffee table and picked up a glass candleholder. Then she threw it against the wall, where it smashed into tiny pieces.

Clea suddenly felt frightened.

"Please calm down," Clea said.

"I want to be the news anchor!"

coffee table	Couchtisch
candleholder	Kerzenständer
I'm sick of...	Ich habe genug davon ...
to come along	daherkommen
to be rid of	los sein
cord	Kabel

Valerie screamed. "I'm sick of watching people like Tessa and Martin get to the top. Tessa was in my way, but I had a chance until you came along, playing detective."

"What do you mean?" Clea asked.

Suddenly Valerie's voice became very soft and quiet. "I thought I was rid of you when you went over the bridge."

She came closer to Clea. With every step she took, Clea tried to move away, but Valerie followed her.

"Yes," Valerie went on. "I thought you'd drowned."

"You're crazy!" Clea exclaimed. "You tried to run me over with a car!"

She moved towards the phone, but Valerie saw what she was doing. She picked up the phone and pulled it hard. The cord came out of the wall. Then she held the cord in both hands.

"Tessa was easy to get rid of," Valerie said. "I went to her house late that night. Lucky for me, Colin had just been there, too. She made us gin and tonics and told me to calm down. But how could I be calm? For years I watched her push her way to the top. She stole my dream, my career."

"That's not true," said Clea. "Tessa was a wonderful journalist. She worked hard for the news anchor job."

"She had everything I wanted. I hated her," Valerie said.

"You killed her," said Clea, finally understanding.

"Yes," Valerie said. "Now you know. But nobody else will ever find out."

Exercise 16: True or false? Markieren Sie mit richtig ✔ oder falsch – !

1. Bonnie was at a hen party on the night of the murder. ☐

2. Marcus got the documents from Tessa's house. ☐

3. Valerie was jealous of Tessa's success. ☐

4. Valerie was driving the car that nearly killed Clea. ☐

5. Clea realized that Marcus was the murderer. ☐

6. Marcus hit Valerie with a potted plant. ☐

She came towards Clea, the phone cord still in her hands. Clea found herself backed up against the living room wall. There was no way to get past Valerie.

Suddenly the telephone cord was around her neck. She was chok-

| backed up against | mit dem Rücken zu |
| pottery | Keramik |

ing. She tried to push Valerie away, but the woman was stronger. The world started to go black.

At that very moment Valerie collapsed. Clea immediately put her hands up to her neck and tried to breathe again. Valerie was on the floor and around her head were bits of smashed pottery.

There was soil and some kind of plant, too. Clea was confused. Then she looked up and saw Marcus.

He was simply standing there, pale and shaking.

"I hit her on the head with the plant," he said. "I brought it as a gift. I wanted to ask you out for a drink to celebrate. It was lucky that the door was open!"

He was so shocked he couldn't help laughing.

"Good timing!" said Clea. She almost laughed, too.

Then she started to cry.

soil	Erde
gift	Geschenk
unconscious	bewusstlos

Just then, DI Binlow came through the door. She looked at Clea, at Marcus, and at Valerie on the floor. Valerie was still unconscious, with the phone cord in her hands and bits of plant, soil and pottery in her hair.

"This should make a good story," Binlow said. "Who wants to start?"

Final Test

Answers

Glossary

List of Exercises

 # Final Test

Exercise 1: Opposites. Welche Gegenteile gehören zusammen? Ordnen Sie zu!

1. ☐ calm   **a)** amazing
2. ☐ damp   **b)** lose
3. ☐ refreshed   **c)** frightened
4. ☐ ordinary   **d)** exhausted
5. ☐ obtain   **e)** dry

Exercise 2: Questions about the text. Beantworten Sie die Fragen zu den 3 Krimis auf Englisch!

1. What happened to Mr Dalton?

_____

2. Where is the Larkins' Bed & Breakfast?

_____

3. Why did Jack Wise hate Phillip Hanson?

_____

4. Who strangled Tessa and why?

_____

Exercise 3: Idiomatic expressions. Was bedeuten die folgenden Ausdrücke? Kreuzen Sie an!

1. Larkin pulled the trigger.

   a) ☐ Larkin tried to shoot with a gun.

   b) ☐ Larkin quickly closed the door of his van.

2. You won't get away with it.

   a) ☐ I will catch you soon.

   b) ☐ You did something wrong and you will be punished for it.

3. Our room has an en suite bathroom.

   a) ☐ We have a bathroom of our own that is joined to our room.

   b) ☐ Our bathroom is as large as a suite.

Exercise 4: Verb forms. Setzen Sie die korrekte Verbform ein!

1. DI Rush `sit` _____ in front of the computer every day.

2. "Have you `hear` _____ the news?" he asks.

3. When Hanson `see` _____ the two detectives, he stops.

4. Clea heard her parents `come` _____ up the stairs to her flat.

5. I `watch` _____ you, I know where you live.

Exercise 5: Crossword puzzle. Lösen Sie das Kreuzworträtsel!

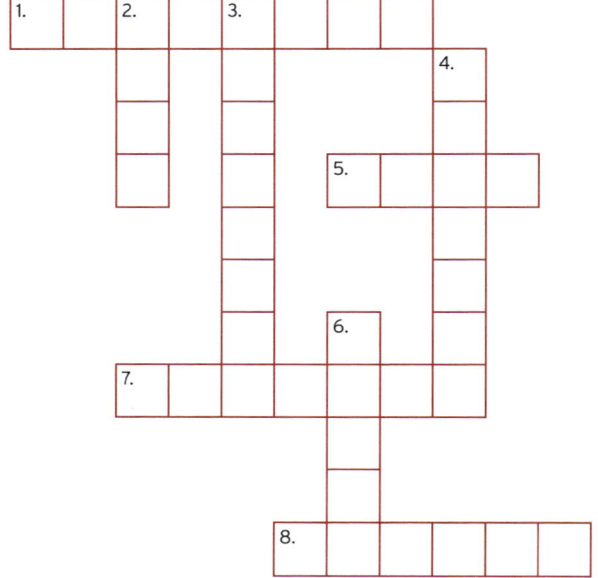

Across

1. The adjective of "horror"
5. To move your hand in the air to attract attention
7. a ceremony for burying a dead person
8. you put these on to avoid leaving fingerprints

Down

2. Sally speaks very fast as if she is in a ...
3. To start a car you put the key into the ...
4. More than two, some
6. the sound that an angry dog makes

Exercise 6: Translation. Übersetzen Sie!

1. unconscious _____
2. memory _____
3. career _____
4. freeze _____
5. folder _____
6. research _____
7. permission _____
8. tell the truth _____

Exercise 7: Translation quiz. Übersetzen Sie und enträtseln Sie das Lösungswort!

1. Motiv   ☐ _ _ _ _ _
2. Verdächtiger   _ ☐ _ _ _ _ _
3. Beerdigung   _ _ _ _ ☐ _ _
4. Tod   ☐ _ _ _ _
5. Zeuge   _ _ _ _ ☐ _ _
6. bedrohen   _ _ ☐ _ _ _ _
7. Geheimnis   _ _ _ ☐ _
8. Affäre   _ _ _ _ _ ☐

Lösung: _ _ _ _ _ _ _ _

 **Answers**

Blood and Breakfast

Exercise 1: 1. true 2. false (They are travelling by car.)
3. false (They will go to a classical concert at Leeds Castle.)
4. false (DI Rush looks younger than he is and he is good-looking.)
5. true 6. false (They used to do Aikido together.)
7. false (Leeds Castle has nothing to do with the city of Leeds.)

Exercise 2: 1. They have travelled by car.
2. She shakes his hand reluctantly because it is dirty.
3. Mrs Larkin comes out of the kitchen.
4. He says that he works in a bank.
5. She is making the evening meal.
6. Brutus is the dog owned by the Larkins; he is a Rottweiler.

Exercise 3: 1. our 2. furniture 3. yard 4. pie 5. case

Exercise 4: 1. fried egg 2. mushroom 3. add 4. gun 5. tray
6. complain 7. tidy

Exercise 5: 1. d 2. e 3. b 4. c 5. a

Exercise 6: 1. He likes Brenda's cooking.
2. They follow him through the door.
3. She serves it in silence.
4. He goes to Ramsgate with her.

Exercise 7:   1. sounds 2. owl 3. go back 4. quiet 5. van
6. Probably

Exercise 8:   1. opens 2. barn 3. feet 4. hurts 5. sure
6. window 7. tired

Exercise 9:   1. began 2. tied 3. shot 4. looked 5. said
6. did 7. came 8. pushed 9. saw 10. had
11. put 12. knew

Exercise 10:   1. cannot 2. at 3. her 4. carefully 5. silent
6. it 7. no 8. Will

Exercise 11:   1. surprised 2. complain 3. drum 4. injure
5. grubby 6. barn 7. unpack 8. eventually
9. ponytail
Lösung: immigrant

Exercise 12:   1. a 2. b 3. a 4. c

Exercise 13:   1. mouth 2. daughter 3. talking 4. inspector
5. bullet 6. guns

Exercise 14:   1. prisoner 2. wire 3. unconscious 4. roast
5. choice 6. calm
Lösung: pistol

Death Wish

Exercise 1:   1. Beweismittel 2. Irrer 3. Anspannung
4. Versuch 5. Opfer 6. kleben

Exercise 2:   1. door 2. mood 3. constable 4. building site
5. emotion 6. competitor

Exercise 3:   1. work 2. money 3. stay 4. children
5. became 6. looking 7. course

Exercise 4:   1. slams 2. earn 3. wanted 4. left

Exercise 5: 1. false (She begins to worry.) 2. true
3. false (Because it might explode.)
4. false (He doesn't want her to go.)
5. true 6. true

Exercise 6: 1. can 2. tell 3. happened 4. Start 5. got up
6. continues 7. indicates 8. will take 9. will go
10. write (down) 11. begins 12. to tell 13. got up
14. ate

Exercise 7: 1. Mr Hanson thought it was a gas explosion.
2. DS Robertshaw is taking the notes.
3. The police is guarding Mr Hanson around
the clock.
4. Detective Superintendent Whipple is leading
the enquiry.

Exercise 8: 1. postman 2. teacher 3. builder 4. policeman
5. joiner

Exercise 9: 1. quiet 2. office 3. happened 4. during
5. murderer 6. protect 7. shrugs

Exercise 10: 1. arrive 2. hand 3. Before 4. opened 5. in 6. is
7. nothing 8. dead

Exercise 11: 1. d 2. g 3. f 4. a 5. b 6. e 7. c

Exercise 12: 1. nodded 2. died 3. thought 4. saw 5. told
6. shut 7. examined 8. cut

Exercise 13: 1. sits 2. works 3. collected 4. is reading 5. is
6. heard 7. has sold

Exercise 14: 1. Mr Hanson wants to emigrate to Brazil.
2. The police found a letter in Wise's pocket.
3. He is now going to prison for twenty-five
years.
4. The inspector wants to arrest Hanson.
5. Both men get out of the car.

Exercise 15: 1. evidence 2. wrist 3. chest 4. stab
5. fingerprint 6. attempt 7. suspect
Lösung: victims

Strangled

Exercise 1: 1. rang 2. came 3. felt 4. found 5. knew
6. left 7. made 8. stood 9. told 10. wrote

Exercise 2: 1. Everything 2. station 3. chairs 4. minutes
5. drunk

Exercise 3: 1. taken 2. needed 3. everyone 4. good
5. everything

Exercise 4: 1. b 2. c 3. a

Exercise 5: 1. through (throu) 2. same (any) 3. university
(universitie) 4. found (founds) 5. with (witch)
6. two (too)

Exercise 6: 1. She asks Martin about the secret information.
2. She hoped to get a current affairs show.
3. She finds it in Tessa's bag.
4. She rings Tessa's friend Maura.
5. Bonnie wrote the threatening emails.

Exercise 7: 1. innocent 2. murderer 3. Perhaps 4. prison
5. real 6. saying

Exercise 8: 1. d 2. f 3. e 4. a 5. b 6. c

Exercise 9: 1. false (She takes the bus.)
2. true
3. false (She is short and thin.)
4. true
5. false (Tessa didn't really like Valerie.)
6. true

Exercise 10:	1. a 2. b 3. b
Exercise 11:	1. dangerous 2. end 3. lose 4. internationally 5. all 6. go 7. asked
Exercise 12:	1. are meeting 2. is catching 3. am thinking 4. are waiting 5. is hitting
Exercise 13:	1. about 2. friend 3. nothing 4. truth 5. documents 6. computer
Exercise 14:	1. crime 2. whisper 3. wave 4. properly 5. unskilled 6. worry
Exercise 15:	1. plants 2. women 3. stories 4. information 5. colleagues 6. gin and tonics 7. pieces 8. bushes
Exercise 16:	1. true 2. false (Marcus has the originals at home.) 3. true 4. true 5. false (She realized Valerie was the murderer.) 6. true

Final Test

Exercise 1:	1. c 2. e 3. d 4. a 5. b
Exercise 2:	1. Mr Larkin shot him and put him in the boot of his car. 2. The Bed & Breakfast is at the coast in Kent. 3. He hated Hanson because Hanson hadn't paid him for his work. 4. Valerie Findlay strangled her, because she was jealous of Tessa.
Exercise 3:	1. a 2. b 3. a
Exercise 4:	1. sits 2. heard 3. sees 4. come 5. am watching

Exercise 5:

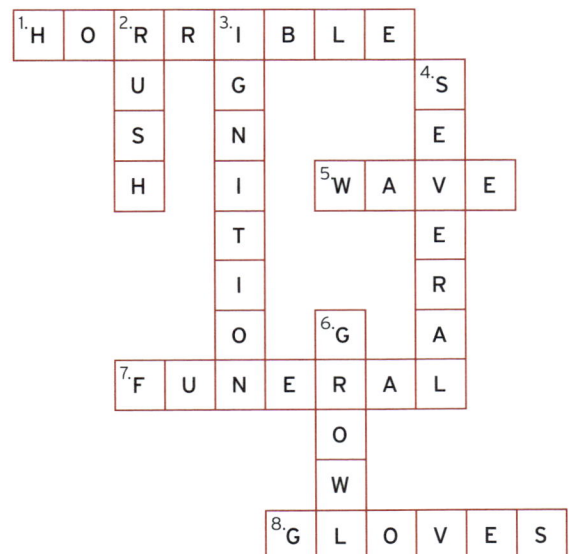

Exercise 6: 1. bewusstlos 2. Erinnerung 3. Karriere
4. frieren 5. Mappe, Ordner 6. Forschung
7. Erlaubnis 8. die Wahrheit sagen

Exercise 7: 1. motive 2. suspect 3. funeral 4. death
5. witness 6. threaten 7. secret 8. affair
Lösung: murderer

# Glossary

absolutely	*hier*: ganz genau
account	Konto
to add	hinzufügen
to admire	bewundern
adult education college	Volkshochschule
after all	doch, letzten Endes
after dark	nach Einbruch der Dunkelheit
all at once	alle gleichzeitig
amazing	erstaunlich
ankle	Fußknöchel
to answer the phone	ans Telefon gehen, abheben
apart from	außer, abgesehen von
apparently	anscheinend
to appear	(er)scheinen
appointment book	Terminplaner
to approach	sich nähern
around the clock	rund um die Uhr
to arrest sb.	jmd. verhaften
art	Kunst
attempt	Versuch
to avoid	vermeiden
backed up against	mit dem Rücken zu
bandage	Verband, Bandage

bar	*hier*: Riegel
barn	Scheune
bay	Bucht
to be (was, been) about	*hier*: in der Gegend sein
to beat (beat, beaten)	schlagen
to be at stake	auf dem Spiel stehen
to be free to …	jmd. freistehen zu …
to beg	bitten, betteln
behaviour	Verhalten
to be involved	beteiligt sein, verwickelt sein
to believe	glauben
belt	Gürtel
to be questioned	verhört werden
to be rid of	los sein
to be right-handed	Rechtshänder(in) sein
blow	Schlag
body	*hier*: Leiche
boot	*hier*: Kofferraum
brave	mutig, tapfer
to break the story	die Nachricht publik machen
to break up with sb.	mit jmd. Schluss machen
to breathe	atmen
building site	Baustelle
bullet	Kugel
bunch	Strauß, Bund
burst of energy	Energieschub
busy	beschäftigt
candleholder	Kerzenständer
to care	sich sorgen, betroffen sein
career	Karriere
to carry out	*hier*: in die Tat umsetzen
cautiously	vorsichtig
certain kinds *pl*	bestimmte Sorten
chance of survival	Überlebenschance
chemistry	Chemie
chest	Brust
Chief Constable	Polizeipräsident(in)
chilling	abschreckend, schrecklich
choice	Wahl

to choke	ersticken
to claim	behaupten
to clatter	klappern
to clear the table	den Tisch abräumen
close(ly)	eng
cloth	Tuch, Lappen
clue	Hinweis, Spur
cobbled	mit Kopfsteinpflaster
coffee table	Couchtisch
to collapse	zusammenbrechen
colleague	Kollege/Kollegin
to come along	daherkommen
to come up behind sb.	hinter jmd. treten
company	Gesellschaft; Unternehmen
competitor	Konkurrent(in)
to complain	sich beklagen
to confess	gestehen
confused	verwirrt
connection	Verbindung
control room	Zentrale
convenient	günstig, praktisch
to convince	überzeugen, überreden
cord	Kabel
court	*hier*: Gericht
crime	Verbrechen
crime scene	Tatort
curious	neugierig
current	Strömung
current affairs show	Nachrichtenmagazin
customer	Kunde/Kundin
damp	feucht
dangerous	gefährlich
dart	Wurfpfeil
to deal with sth.	sich kümmern um
to deny	leugnen, abstreiten
to destroy	kaputtmachen
Detective Superintendent	Hauptkommissar(in)
to dial	wählen, anrufen
to disappear	verschwinden

to disturb	durcheinander bringen
Do as you please.	Mach was du willst.
doorway	Türöffnung
to do sb. a favour	jmd. einen Gefallen tun
doubt	Zweifel
Do you need a ride?	Soll ich dich mitnehmen?
to drag	schleppen
drawer	Schublade
dressing	*hier*: Verband
to drown	ertrinken
drum	Trommel
to earn	verdienen
ecosystem	Ökosystem
edge	Rand
effort	Anstrengung, Einsatz
elderly	ältere(r), betagt
emergency	Notfall
to emigrate	auswandern
encouragement	Ermutigung
to end up	(schließlich) enden, landen
English Channel	Ärmelkanal
enjoyable	vergnüglich
enquiry	Ermittlung, Untersuchung
en suite bathroom	eigenes Bad
entry phone	Gegensprechanlage
environment	Umwelt
especially	besonders
eventually	schließlich
evidence	Beweismittel
to examine	untersuchen
except for	außer, abgesehen von
to exclaim	ausrufen
explosives *pl*	Sprengstoff
fairground	Rummelplatz
false	falsch, gefälscht
familiar	bekannt, vertraut
to fasten	befestigen
to feel uncomfortable	sich unwohl fühlen
ferry	Fähre

to fetch	abholen
file	Akte
to find sb. guilty	jmd. für schuldig erklären
fingerprint	Fingerabdruck
to flow	fließen
folder	Mappe, Ordner
forensic science laboratory	kriminaltechnisches Labor
freezing cold	eiskalt
fried egg	Spiegelei
to frighten	erschrecken, ängstigen
frightened	verängstigt
funeral	Beerdigung
garage	*hier*: (Kfz-)Werkstatt
to gasp	keuchen, nach Luft schnappen
genuine	wirklich, echt
to get a good night's sleep	durchschlafen
to get away with sth.	mit etw. davonkommen
to get to one's feet	aufstehen
gift	Geschenk
glove	Handschuh
glue	Klebstoff
to go (went, gone) on	*hier*: fortfahren
gorgeous	herrlich, wunderschön
to go (went, gone) to court	vor Gericht ziehen
to go (went, gone) up to sb.	auf jmd. zugehen
government	Regierung
to grab	greifen, packen
grim	grimmig, ernst
to growl	knurren
grubby	dreckig, schmuddelig
to grunt	grunzen, grummeln
guilty	schuldig
gunshot	(Gewehr-)Schuss
hall	Flur
to handle	anfassen, umgehen mit
handsome	attraktiv, gutaussehend
hardly	kaum
to hate	hassen
headquarters	Zentrale, Hauptquartier

to head straight for	direkt zusteuern auf
ϟ hen party	Junggesellinnenabschied
to hire	anheuern, beauftragen
to hit (hit, hit)	*hier*: aufschlagen auf
home-made	selbst gebaut, selbst gemacht
horrible	schrecklich
huge argument	heftiger Streit
huge	riesig
to hug	umarmen
hunted	gejagt
ϟ Hiya. (How are you.)	Hallo, wie geht's.
ignition	Zündung
to imagine	sich vorstellen
immediately	sofort
impatiently	ungeduldig
impolite	unhöflich
impression	Eindruck
I'm sick of…	Ich habe genug davon …
in an instant	in einem Augenblick
in a rush	in Eile, eilig
incident room	Einsatzzentrale
indeed	wirklich, in der Tat
to indicate	(an)zeigen
injured	verletzt
innocent	unschuldig
in person	persönlich
to insist	beharren
insurance company	Versicherungsgesellschaft
insurance policy	Versicherungspolice
to insure sb.	jmd. versichern
intention	Absicht
to interview	befragen
to investigate	ermitteln, untersuchen
investigation	Ermittlung, Untersuchung
investigator	Ermittler(in)
to involve sb.	jmd. verwickeln in
Is anything the matter?	Stimmt etwas nicht?
it's my fault	es ist meine Schuld
jealousy	Eifersucht

jewellery	Schmuck
job interview	Vorstellungsgespräch
to join sb.	sich zu jmd. gesellen
to join sth.	etw. beitreten
joiner	Tischler(in)
junk mail	(unerwünschte) Werbepost
just	*hier*: gerade eben
just in time	gerade (noch) rechtzeitig
to keep doing sth.	weitermachen mit
landscape	Landschaft
lane	schmaler Weg, Gasse
leather	Leder
liquid	Flüssigkeit
lounge	Wohnzimmer
low	*hier*: leise, gedämpft
luxury	Luxus, luxuriös
madman, -men *pl*	Irrer
to make sth. public	etw. publik machen, etw. veröffent- lichen
married	verheiratet
meanwhile	währenddessen
medical record	Krankenakte
memory	Erinnerung
mood	Stimmung, Laune
mortuary	Leichenhalle
movement	Bewegung
mud	Schlamm
to mumble	murmeln
to murder	ermorden
murder	Mord
murder case	Mordfall
murderer	Mörder(in)
mushroom	Pilz
news anchor	Nachrichtenmoderator(in)
news presenter	Nachrichtensprecher(in)
to obtain	erhalten, sich verschaffen
obviously	offensichtlich
off balance	aus dem Gleichgewicht
offer	Angebot

officer	*hier*: Polizist(in); Beamte(r)
official	Beamte(r), Offizielle(r)
opportunity	Gelegenheit
ornament	Ziergegenstand
over and over	immer wieder
to overpower	überwältigen
owl	Eule
pain	Schmerz
pale	blass
paramedic	Sanitäter(in)
to pass	*hier*: vergehen
pebble	Kieselstein
permission	Erlaubnis
pile	Stapel
plant	Pflanze
to plead	flehen
pleasant	erfreulich
pleased	erfreut
poached	pochiert
poacher	Wilderer
to point (to)	zeigen (auf), richten (auf)
police record	Vorstrafenregister
ponytail	Pferdeschwanz
pool	*hier*: Lache
to post	per Post schicken, einwerfen
pottery	Keramik
to pour	(ein)gießen
presumably	vermutlich
previous	vorherig, vorausgegangen
prison	Gefängnis
prisoner	Gefangene(r)
processing plant	Verarbeitungsanlage
professional	*hier*: Akademiker(in)
proof	Beweis
properly	richtig
to protect	(be)schützen
protection	Schutz, Bewachung
proudly	stolz
to provide	*hier*: abstellen (Polizist)

to pull over	*hier*: an den Straßenrand fahren
to pull sb. along	*hier*: jmd. mitreißen
to put out one's hand	die Hand ausstrecken
to put up a struggle	sich wehren
quarry	Steinbruch
rabbit	Kaninchen
radio signal	Funksignal
to reach (out)	greifen (nach)
to realize	erkennen, sich bewusst werden
to receive	bekommen, erhalten
to recognize	(wieder)erkennen
to redden	rot werden
to reduce	verringern, reduzieren
refreshed	erfrischt; erholt
relieved	erleichtert
reluctantly	widerwillig
to remark	anmerken
to remember	sich erinnern
to remove	abziehen, entfernen
request	Wunsch
to research	(er)forschen
research	Forschung
revenge	Rache
right away	sofort, gleich
ringing noise	Klingelgeräusch
risk	Risiko
riverbank	Flussufer
roast	gebraten
to run (ran, run) (a business)	(einen Betrieb) führen
to run the company	das Unternehmen leiten
to rush past	schnell vorbeiziehen
satisfaction	Zufriedenheit, Genugtuung
scarf	Schal
scientist	Wissenschaftler(in)
to scowl	ein mürrisches Gesicht machen
scream	Schrei
to seem as though	scheinen als ob
serious(ly)	ernst

to set (set, set)	*hier*: stellen
to set (set, set) off	sich auf den Weg machen, aufbrechen
settee	Sofa
several	einige
to shake (shook, shaken)	*hier*: zittern
to shake hands	sich die Hand geben
shape	Form, Umrisse
she felt sick	ihr war übel
she wasn't feeling like it	ihr war nicht danach (zumute)
short-sleeved	kurzärmelig
⚡ to show (showed, shown) up	auftauchen
to shrug one's shoulders	die Achseln zucken
silence	Stille
to slam the door	die Tür zuschlagen
to slash	aufschlitzen
slaughterhouse	Schlachthof
to slide (slid, slid)	gleiten (lassen)
slightly	etwas, ein wenig
slim	schlank
to slip	ausrutschen
to smash	zerschlagen
smooth	glatt
to snarl	knurren
to sob	schluchzen
soil	Erde
solicitor	Anwalt/Anwältin
sourly	griesgrämig
to stab	erstechen
stall	Stand
statement	Aussage
steep	steil
to stick (stuck, stuck)	kleben
straight	gerade
straight away	direkt, sofort
strange(ly)	seltsam
strangled	erdrosselt, erwürgt
strength	Kraft, Stärke

to strike (struck, struck)	zuschlagen
to struggle	kämpfen; sich winden
struggle	Kampf
stubborn	stur
sudden rush	plötzlicher Anfall
to suggest	nahelegen
to suit sb.	(zu) jmd. passen
to suppose	annehmen
surprised	überrascht
to suspect	verdächtigen
suspect	Verdächtige(r)
suspicious	misstrauisch; verdächtig
to swallow	hinunterschlucken
to swear (swore, sworn)	*hier*: fluchen
to switch on/off	an-/ausschalten
tension	Anspannung
Thank goodness.	Gott sei Dank.
thatched	reetgedeckt
the jury	die Geschworenen
to threaten	drohen, bedrohen
threatening letter	Drohbrief
tidy	ordentlich
to tidy up	aufräumen
to tie	binden
tiny	winzig
tissue	Papiertuch
to your face	in jds. Angesicht
tray	Tablett
to tremble	zittern
trial	Prozess, (Gerichts-)Verfahren
to trust sb.	jmd. vertrauen
truth	Wahrheit
to turn pale	blass werden, erblassen
to type in	eintippen
tyre	Reifen
unconscious	bewusstlos
under arrest	festgenommen
to underestimate	unterschätzen
uneven	uneben

unknown	unbekannt
unlike	anders als, im Unterschied zu
to unlock	aufschließen
to unpack	auspacken
upright	aufrecht
to upset (upset, upset)	(ver)ärgern, aufregen
upset	aufgebracht, aufgeregt
van	Lieferwagen
vegetarian	Vegetarier(in)
very good	sehr wohl! *veraltet*
victim counselling	Opferberatung
victim	Opfer
view	Aussicht; Sicht
violence	Gewalttätigkeit
to wait and see	abwarten
to waste	verschwenden
to wave	winken, schwenken
What's the matter?	Was ist los?
will	*hier*: Testament
wire	Draht
wiry	drahtig
with all one's heart	von ganzem Herzen
witness	Zeuge/Zeugin
to wonder	sich fragen
wrist	Handgelenk
yard	Hof
to yawn	gähnen
to yell	schreien, rufen
You don't want to …	Du solltest nicht …

List of Exercises

Lernkrimi Lektüren Englisch

Lernkrimi Lektüren Englisch

B2

Bloody Diamonds
Classic
ISBN 978-3-8174-9494-1

Nobody Dies Twice
Classic
ISBN 978-3-8174-9495-8

In Terror
Lernthriller
ISBN 978-3-8174-8857-5

C1

A Scottish Murder Mystery
Classic
ISBN 978-3-8174-8379-2

Keep Calm and Carry On Killing
Classic
ISBN 978-3-8174-1644-8

Lernkrimi Comic Englisch

A1

Chasing Bloody Mary
ISBN 978-3-8174-1655-4

Lernkrimi Sprachkurs Englisch

A1/A2

Lernkrimi Sprachkurs
ISBN 978-3-8174-7844-5

Lernkrimi Hörbücher Englisch

 A1

Black Wedding
ISBN 978-3-8174-1817-6

Dangerous Deals
ISBN 978-3-8174-9988-5

 A2

A Shot in the Night
ISBN 978-3-8174-8202-3

The Butterworth Mystery
ISBN 978-3-8174-8203-0

Death Wish
ISBN 978-3-8174-8204-7

Strangled
ISBN 978-3-8174-1876-3

 B1

Bloody Revenge
ISBN 978-3-8174-8860-5

Bloody Legacy
ISBN 978-3-8174-7676-3

B2

Crime & Company
ISBN 978-3-8174-8976-3

Murder at the Office
ISBN 978-3-8174-7747-0

Lernkrimi Rätselblöcke Englisch

 A1

Murderous Games
ISBN 978-3-8174-9500-9

 A2

The Art of Crime
ISBN 978-3-8174-9155-1

 B1

A Deadly Puzzle
ISBN 978-3-8174-8832-2

Englisch lernen für geübte Anfänger

ISBN 978-3-8174-8202-3

Spannendes Hörerlebnis

Der in diesem Band enthaltene
Kurzkrimi **Blood and Breakfast** jetzt auch
als Hörbuch:
Audio-CD mit Begleitbuch
Gelesen von Muttersprachlern
Ca. 60 Minuten packender Krimispaß

Weitere Lernkrimi Hörbücher aus
diesem Band:
Death Wish
(ISBN 978-3-8174-8204-7)
Strangled
(ISBN 978-3-8174-1876-3)

ISBN 978-3-8174-1764-3

Übung macht den Meister

Das Übungsbuch ist ideal für geübte
Anfänger und Wiedereinsteiger, die
ihre Englischkenntnisse auffrischen und
vertiefen möchten.

Rund 200 thematisch sortierte Übungen zu
Wortschatz und Grammatik

Inklusive Infokästen, Lösungen und
Glossar im Anhang

Extra: Krimilektüre für geübte Anfänger – so
wird das Sprachtraining noch spannender!

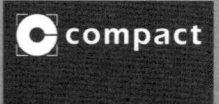